You are My Boro: The Unlikely Small Town in Europe

By Christopher Combe

You Are My Boro? The Unlikely Adventures of a Small Town in Europe

ISBN: 978-1-4710-0664-7

About the Author

Christopher Combe was born in Berwick-upon-Tweed and spent much of his childhood living in various locations around Germany and the UK, before attending a North Yorkshire boarding school in the 1980s.

On leaving school, Chris settled in the North Yorkshire area, finding work as a quantity surveyor. His continued desire to travel and see new places has taken him to the USA, the Far East and the Arabian Gulf.

Chris has had an interest in reading and writing since an early age, with horror and sci-fi featuring strongly. In recent years he has blogged on a regular basis and contributed to football fanzine websites.

Chris now lives in a small market town in North Yorkshire with his wife and two children. His first book, "One Year In Wonderland: A True Tale of Expat Life in Dubai" came out in July 2011.

To Dad, with due apologies.

Preface

(The Confessions of a Middle-Class, Part-Time Glory Supporter)

Before I launch myself into telling the story of Boro's Golden Decade and a Bit (1995 to 2006) from my point of view, I feel that I need to get a few things off my chest. Let's call it a confessional, for the sake of argument. If, after reading these shameful admissions, you think I am a feckless and unforgiveable sinner who should be cast into the hellish wastelands of Sunderland, then that's fine. Put the book or the e-reader down right away, give your shiny halos a quick rub and then go out and check your glass houses for broken panes. If, on the other hand, you can live with these little foibles, then please continue and - I hope - enjoy the ride.

Let's start with number one, which I know can be an issue for quite a few people: I am probably what you'd call "Middle Class". I didn't choose to be, but that's where I've ended up in my life. I was born to "Working Class" parents, but they took certain career choices and had some luck along the way, giving me the chances they never had. I've tried not to squander these opportunities too badly, and now I could never, ever class myself as Working Class, even if I do eat eggy bread and still call the latest meal of the day "tea". Yes, I went to a boarding school – it wasn't private, it was a state Grammar school, an important distinction – but I was looked down upon when I first went there school by the sons of high-ranking Forces officers and diplomats. By the time I left to find a job at the tender and testosterone-fuelled age of 18 I spoke with a "posh" accent and had all the streetwise acumen of a circus lion suddenly released into an African wildlife reserve. So, accept this and be at peace with it, if you possibly can: I am Middle Class and I am writing about the apparently Working Class game of Association Football.

Second confession: I am, for want of a better word, a Glory Supporter. Now, this comes with even more qualifications than number one, because in simple terms a Glory Supporter is usually defined as someone who chooses to support a successful team like Manchester United or Chelsea when they used to support Burnley or Watford, for instance. I went the other way, choosing to change from being a childhood Manchester United fan to a Middlesbrough supporter in my early adult years. So technically, I am actually an Anti-

Glory Supporter. The reasons for this are set out in detail in the early chapters of the following book, but to put it in a nutshell, it's down to my nomadic and regularly uprooted early life, which left me without a sense of home and belonging that may have just been offered by a football team local to where I ended up living twenty-odd years ago. Something like that, without wanting to veer into mawkish and maudlin amateur psychology.

My third and final horrible confession is one that may just be the straw that breaks the camel's, donkey's and elephant's back for some readers. I'm only a part-timer. I don't follow Boro home and away and I never have. I had a season ticket for three or four seasons, but gave it up when work and family commitments took priority in my life, and even when I did have a season ticket I didn't go to any away games, unless you count cup semi-finals and finals at neutral venues. I'm no superfan and have never claimed to be. I don't enter such competitions in urinating. I'm just an average supporter who has had a season ticket in the past, has been to many, many matches and who now goes to a few games here and there. Whichever way you look at it I have maintained an avid interest throughout my supportership.

So there you are. Take it or leave it. The horrifying confessions are out and my soul is laid bare. I don't apologise for anything, and I don't ask for forgiveness or mercy. It's entirely possible that I'm making this confession to myself as much as anyone else, but I just want people to read the story and know without any shred of doubt the kind of eyes they are looking through. I have a lazy eye, mind, so pop on some thick NHS spectacles with plaster over the right lens and away we shall go.

Let's go for a ride…

Chapter 1 - 1970 - 1989

Before Boro

Nobody chooses to support the Boro; you are born to it.

I've lost count of how many times I've heard or read this phrase since I started following the fortunes of Middlesbrough Football Club. I know it's not strictly true, but I rarely argue the toss with anyone who says it. It's one of those generalisations with *some* foundation, but which isn't completely accurate. The truest part of it is that people do not choose to support Middlesbrough FC in the same way they might choose to support the likes of Manchester United, Chelsea or Liverpool.

The vast majority of people who support the club either hail from the Teesside area or have parents from there. They have been brought up with the belief that only one football team in the world matters, above even the national team. In many cases this indoctrination sticks fast. Of course, there are kids from the area who decide, in defiance of family and friends, to support the more glamorous, successful clubs and who wear their replica kits at every opportunity. For these parents whose children go against their grain, there is still the hope that they might grow out of being a "glory supporter" and start following their hometown club. On the flip side of the coin, I can't imagine you would find many children in the playgrounds of Toxteth, Salford or Acton wearing Boro strips, unless of course they have parents from Teesside or have moved from there.

I am probably classed as a very rare breed, and I don't mean a middle class liberal living in a North Yorkshire market town. I am a Boro supporter who isn't from Teesside, and who wasn't compelled to support them through parental example. I was born in the most northerly town in England where the local team play in the Scottish Third Division and where the accent is more Jock than Geordie, but you will still see England flags being flown during the World Cup. Somehow - I think fortuitously - I ended up becoming a supporter of Middlesbrough in the mid-1990s. I became an anti-glory supporter, for want of a better term, and personally speaking, I think I jumped on the Boro rollercoaster just at the right time, just as it was about to climb into the dizzying, rarefied air of what - for the Boro - was the stratosphere.

If anyone's to blame for this (if indeed anyone *needs* to be blamed for it), it's probably the man from the Army careers office who came to see my father when he was wondering what to do with his life. He was at a point where he had narrowed the options down to either life as a policeman or a career as a soldier. The Army sent a man to talk to him; the police didn't, so my dad joined up and went off to Catterick for training, and before long his young family was moving to West Germany. I only lived in the town of my birth for just over two years, and soon became accustomed to a nomadic existence, moving to a new posting every three years. Most of the next seventeen years was spent living in various places in Germany, punctuated by secondary education in a North Yorkshire boarding school and two short postings to UK bases.

My father was a football fan (Manchester United were his team; he began following them in the late '50s during the era of Busby's Babes and Duncan Edwards) and he gave me my first live taste of the beautiful game in the divided city of Berlin in the late 1970s. I had watched some of the '78 World Cup on our tiny colour television, but this viewing experience was completely and utterly transcended when my father took me to watch Hertha Berlin playing SC Hamburg at the huge Olympic Stadium in Berlin. I was immediately captivated by the scale of everything. Attending such a grand occasion and being surrounded by so many people was quite overwhelming at the age of eight or nine, especially when it's in such an historic and frankly vast venue. I wasn't afraid; I just sat on the narrow bench seat and watched the game with growing fascination, listening to the moans, groans, shouts and cheers of a football crowd. I enjoyed my cold half-time bockwurst served in stale bread and just absorbed every single minute of actually being there, completely immersed in it rather than just watching it on a little flickering screen. Kevin Keegan played for Hamburg, I remember, and with his hairstyle was easily identifiable, even from high up in the stands. I think he scored in the match as well.

When we moved to different places with the various postings, we endeavoured to find a local team to watch, be it a top flight professional club or a semi-pro outfit playing to small crowds in a tiny stadium. Televised football was quite a rare event in those days, as opposed to the wall-to-wall coverage we enjoy today, especially matches from the English Football League, in the days when it was Divisions One to Four. The British Forces Broadcasting Service (BFBS) linked up with the Radio 2 Saturday afternoon coverage, so we managed to hear the results and catch the occasional commentary of a United game.

During my time at boarding school in England I managed to see some of those rare televised games in the days of ITV's Big Match when it was presented by the likes of Jim Rosenthal. There was always a big crowd in the boarding house TV room for the FA Cup Finals and World Cup Finals games. I remember the buzz of Cup Final days, with the coverage starting around noon on one or even both main channels with the teams arriving and walking on the pitch in their best bib and tucker; the early summer sun blazing in a brilliant blue sky, the military band marching and playing on the pristine Wembley pitch and the singing of Abide With Me. It was a real occasion that took up half of the day.

There were some cracking finals in the '80s: Manchester United v Brighton, "Smith must score," and the resulting, one-sided replay, Everton v Watford, Manchester United beating Everton with Norman Whiteside's wonder goal in extra time after Kevin Moran's sending-off, Coventry v Spurs and Houchen's diving header; Wimbledon's Crazy Gang beating the mighty Liverpool; too many memories, and more than just a handful of teams competing. It's a shame the cancerous undercurrent of hooliganism was still a significant problem. I remember the news footage from the Luton against Millwall game where seats were ripped off and hurled all over the shop like large Scrabble tiles. It is annoying when you get too many vowels, admittedly. I have some more pleasant, vivid memories of the 1986 World Cup Finals in Mexico, with the pitches permanently bathed in sunshine and England's valiant effort after the dreadful start in the group stages. That quarter final against Argentina lives long in the memory: the Hand of Cheeky Get, Maradona's sublime second goal and the Barnes-inspired fight-back. I can still see Lineker lunging for and just missing that second cross. It was agonising.

Every football fan over a certain age knows that the '80s is now recognized as a watershed decade for the game. The decrepit, ageing stadiums with their fenced-in, crumbling terracing were a disgrace, and change was inevitable. The disasters at Heysel and Bradford raised questions – people going to watch a game of football shouldn't be dying – but the horrors of Hillsborough were the final straw for the public and for the authorities. Hooliganism was not an excuse for herding people through small entrances into what were effectively cages. These were humans, not animals. Something had to change. The resulting Taylor Report changed the face of the game, forcing the clubs to redevelop their grounds, and subsequently changing the demographic of the football-viewing public as admission prices inevitably rose to fund the improvements.

My dad's final posting was to Catterick in North Yorkshire in 1989, the same year I left school. I entered the wonderful world of working for a wage, finding gainful employment with a steel fabrication firm in Darlington where I made cups of tea and stared dumbly at a black and green computer screen. I passed my driving test and got a car (a beaten-up, blue Mk III Escort). I met a local lass and got engaged (it didn't last; she was slightly unhinged). A year later the recession took hold and the company shed a third of the workforce. I was one of the unlucky third, but did have more luck when I managed to find another job fairly quickly with an engineering firm in Middlesbrough. Someone in Darlington put a good word in for me.

I ended up working in Teesside for the next decade, and ended up living there after I got married in 1995. But back in 1990, the year Gazza ended up in floods of tears in that ill-fated World Cup semi-final against the Germans, the fates were shifting and the first seeds were being sown.

Chapter 2 - 1990 - 1995

Sowing The Seeds of Boro.

Until I started working in Middlesbrough, I'll be honest and say that Boro hadn't really registered with me. I knew there was a football team there who were rivals with Sunderland and Newcastle. I also knew they were seen as something of a yo-yo team that played in an old-fashioned, dilapidated stadium set amongst rows of terraced houses. I even remember their exciting cup ties with Everton in the '80s with all the replays and late goal drama. But that was essentially that.

I was a Manchester United fan back then, following on from my dad. I say fan rather than supporter quite deliberately, because I almost always watched or listened from afar. I attended very few games of theirs other than the odd cup tie here and there. I remember one match at Newcastle in 1990 where I went in the home end with my Dad and brother and couldn't believe the racist abuse being hurled at Manchester United's black players. I also went to a United game at Sunderland's Roker Park with work colleagues in the name of client entertainment, and was as unimpressed by the Mackems and their frankly unenlightened attitudes as I had been with the Geordies.

I can't say the attachment to the Red Devils was a particularly deep one; more like the loyalty one feels towards a kind of food or a band. Kids like me who lived in many places - army brats, for want of a better term - almost always followed big teams like Manchester United or Liverpool, unless they were Scottish and the choice was between Celtic and Rangers.

Working with Teessiders was a baptism of roaring Wilton flare-stacks. I was a shy, quiet, Grammar-school-educated young man with a Middle Class accent thrown into the deep end of a working environment with people who had a wickedly sharp sense of humour and who pounced on the smallest of foibles in the name of banter and craic. I eventually learned how to give as good as I got and not take it too personally. Eventually. Football banter was always popular, and being a Manchester United fan made me a target for more teasing. I'm sure it would have been ten times worse had I professed a liking for Newcastle.

Either way, I managed to make some good friends, some of who are still good friends now; lads like Gaz, Nick and Marco who enjoyed a laugh at work back in the days when it was possible. We were in some small, Victorian-era offices on Yarm Road in Stockton for a few years before the company moved to horrible, anti-slacker open-plan offices. No more games of Subbuteo or office cricket with a rolled up ball of paper. There was a pizza shop across the road as well, which I had many an unhealthy lunch from. I still blame that pizza shop for helping me put on several stone in the space of a few years. I went drinking with my new mates in the night-spots of Stockton, Boro and Yarm and played (played being a loose description) 5-a-side football with work colleagues at a floodlit pitch in Sedgefield. Despite having a buggered hip I put myself about with no little enthusiasm, trying to close the gap in skill level with lads who'd played the game all the way through school, whereas the only game at my school had been rugger, old bean.

I even played a couple of games of eleven-a-side for the office team in the occasional friendly games that were orgnaised. I had a nightmare time in goal one game, then came on as a comedy sub to play up front and nearly scored after running (or limping very fast) on to a lovely through ball, but the keeper got there just before me and picked the ball up. In the pub after the game the referee obviously failed to recognise me sitting right opposite him when he remarked to members of the opposition, "It's a good job that cripple didn't score at the end, eh?" There ensued a rather awkward silence until I asked him where his guide dog was, as he seemed unable to identify people sitting a few feet away. Oh how we laughed. The bastard.

As time progressed I learned more and more about the area, being in the fortunate position of having to drive around the region to measure utility renewal works and spray yellow paint all over the streets of various towns of the North East. I soon picked up scraps of local history and came to learn about how the juxtaposition of this industrial town and the rugged but beautiful Tees Valley / North Yorkshire countryside came into being. I also learned a lot about the warm, humorously pessimistic people and the passionate rivalries that were held with the other football clubs in the region, picking up references to Mackems, Geordies, Smoggies and so on. I learned about local delicacies like the Parmo, a take-away favourite consisting of a breadcrumb-covered pork escalope smothered in béchamel sauce and a ton of cheap cheese alongside chips and the obligatory healthy salad. I imagine there are several versions of the dish.

I learned how to say "Middlesbrough" properly, not "MiddlesbOrough", even though the team are nick-named Boro rather than Bro. People from other parts of the country tend to struggle with it, especially my father, who still uses the wrong pronunciation, despite my constant corrections.

In terms of Middlesbrough's football club I heard legendary names like George Hardwick, George Camsell, Wilf Mannion and Archie Stephens. I learned that players like Graeme Souness and Craig Johnston had played for Boro before moving on to "bigger" clubs like Liverpool. I heard about the Anglo-Scottish Cup and Jack Charlton's celebrated team of the mid-'70s. I learned that Boro had achieved their best league positions just before both World Wars, and that there was an alleged gypsy curse on Ayresome Park which meant Boro were destined to be perennial losers who had never won a major trophy and probably never would, if you believed some people.

What was impressed upon me was the real attachment local people had to their club. It wasn't like following a franchise; this was deep-rooted and very, very important. The local rivalries with Sunderland and Newcastle were passionate and forceful. I remember catching a hard-fought Boro v Sunderland game on Tyne Tees TV that bore testament to this fact, with the enmity between fans and even players (in the days when local lads were well represented in the teams) being quite evident.

Then there was a bleary night out in Newcastle in 1992 – it was the night Denmark beat Germany in the European Championship Final - when I joined a rabble of work colleagues on a trip up the A19 in a rusting white mini-bus bearing the words BORO TAXIS in giant red lettering. It was the first season of the new Premier League, and whilst Boro were in it, the Geordies were languishing in the Football League waiting for the curly-haired messiah to ride to their rescue, and their crowds were averaging less than 15,000. So much for them always having fantastic support. Anyway, as we entered enemy territory and stopped at a set of traffic lights, the driver spotted a man walking past. He immediately rolled his window down and shouted to the bewildered-looking Geordie: "I bet you wish you were in the Premier League, mate!" Any night that started like that, went on to feature narrowly-avoided fights on crowded dance floors and ended with impromptu swims in the Tyne was going to be memorable as well as educational. This kind of lifestyle was new and more than a little bit scary to me, but the more I heard and saw, the more I wanted to learn.

In the background, big changes were afoot at Middlesbrough FC. The club had gone through a torrid period in the mid-'80s, flirting with complete oblivion in 1986 when the Ayresome Park gates were locked by receivers and the team had to play at Hartlepool's ground. They even had to train in public parks. A young local businessman called Steve Gibson came to the forefront as part of the consortium that saved the club from winding-up, and when he became Chairman, he began putting his unprecedented vision for the club into action.

This ambition was made tangible by the announcement of a new stadium to be built on a patch of redundant industrial land between the A66 and the river. Thin, grey members of steel began to rise from the ground, slowly taking the form of a brand new, 30,000 capacity all-seater stadium. It was the first to be built to the specifications laid out in the Taylor report, and the largest new stadium to be built in the UK for several decades. There was some controversy over the ordering of the steel from Germany rather than from the huge British Steel works just along the A66 at Redcar.

Boro were the pioneers of new stadia; many other clubs would soon follow suit, with the likes of Derby and Sunderland building their own new grounds to similar templates. Derby's Pride Park stadium is almost identical to the Riverside, other than the colour of the seats and a few minor architectural details. These grounds were more suited to the more mobile and affluent modern fan-base, being located out of town rather than in the middle of residential areas. As I drove past the site on the A66 on my way to measure holes in the ground in South Bank or Redcar, I watched with growing interest as the new structures gradually took shape and started looking like a stadium.

It was also hard to miss the way the club were moving in terms of team management and playing personnel, and in the summer of 1994 the Manchester United legend, Bryan Robson, he of Captain-Marvel-with-the-dodgy-shoulder fame, was appointed player-manager of the team. His former team-mate Viv Anderson joined him as Assistant Manager. An all-too-brief stint in the shiny new, much-heralded Premier League during its inaugural 1992-93 season had obviously whetted the appetite, and Gibson wanted to move the club to the next level. Being a yo-yo club was old hat and boring. The new stadium and the new manager were clear signals of intent, and these developments captured mine and probably many others' imaginations.

In the early years of the decade, football was becoming sexy and popular again after the hooliganism-scarred days of the '80s. After doing so well in 1990, England had failed to qualify for the World Cup in '94 under Graham Taylor's disastrous reign, but even the USA was getting in on the act with their razzmatazz soccer extravaganza. TV coverage was becoming more and more widespread, and the airwaves were dominated by new satellite broadcaster Sky TV's adverts featuring the Simple Minds' song *Alive and Kicking*. Britpop and Cool Britannia were just in their infancy, and England would be hosting its own international tournament in a couple of years, which was sure to make football even more popular. The future looked bright for everyone with a stake in the game.

On a Tuesday night in August 1994, I managed to convince my old man to come and watch Boro play Manchester United in a testimonial match for Clayton Blackmore, the Welsh full-back who had followed the new manager from United. We drove up to Middlesbrough and parked in the narrow terraced streets surrounding the compact ground. It was my first taste of Boro live, and my first time inside Ayresome Park. We squeezed in through the narrow, antique turnstiles and made our way up to our seats. The smell of beer, Bovril and tobacco filled the air. We sat high up in the main stand, and when we emerged onto the stands to see the glowing green carpet of the pitch, with the noisy terrace of the Holgate End to our left and the away fans in the East stand to our right, I was impressed. It was very different to the few United games I had been to at Old Trafford. It felt more convivial and more authentic, and there was a definite spark of electricity in the air that night. The expectancy was almost tangible.

The match was well attended and the fans were enthusiastic, but it ended up being little more than a pre-season work-out and an easy 3-0 win for United, who were just at the start of the most successful period in their history under Alex Ferguson. Of course, Boro were also at the start of something, and that night under those bright floodlights, I felt a slight but significant shift in my feelings.

That following season saw these feelings shift more and more. Heightened interest turned into genuine keenness to see games and watch the team's progress. Something special was happening, and it seemed Middlesbrough were destined to play their first season in their new stadium at the top level of English domestic football, back in the Premier League. Boro played their last season at Ayresome Park to increasing crowds and heightening expectations, and promotion was sealed in the last game at the old ground on 30th April, 1995 with a 2-1 win over Luton Town. Naturally there was a party atmosphere, but it was also an emotional farewell to the stadium for the fans who had stuck by the team through the dark days of the last decade. They said goodbye to the Holgate End, the Bob End, the chicken run and all those other pieces of history, but looked forward to a new era in their brand new stadium, the name of which had been decided by a fans' vote: The Riverside Stadium. It was the closing of a chapter in the club's history, but also the opening of a new, exciting episode for Middlesbrough Football Club. It was really just the beginning of the adventure.

Chapter 3 - 1995/96

Robson's Riverside Revolution

1995 was a big year for me as well as for Middlesbrough FC, but there'll be more on that later. This was the year that saw the collapse of the Barings Bank and the arrest of rogue trader Nick Leeson, the Oklahoma City bombing, the farce that was the OJ Simpson trial, the end of the Bosnian war and the arrival on the scene of a new digital medium: DVDs. *Toy Story* was top-grossing film of the year, with *Apollo 13*, *Casino* and *Seven* also placing in the top ten. In music, the Oasis versus Blur battle for domination grabbed the headlines, whilst Coolio's *Gangsta's Paradise* was top-selling single. In the world of sport, a young golfer called Tiger Woods won the US Amateur Championships, Mandela watched South Africa win the Rugby Union World Cup, Michael Schumacher won the Formula One World Championship and Ajax of the Netherlands won the UEFA Champions League.

For Boro and for me, there were big moves and big changes. Boro started the 1995-96 season in their new stadium and back in the Premier League. I married the Yorkshire lass I'd been courting for a while and moved to the magical, hall-of-mirrors landscape of Ingleby Barwick, essentially to be closer to my job working for a firm of quantity surveyors in Stockton-on-Tees. My move north gave me even more of an excuse to follow the team that was slowly, but surely, gaining my admiration and affection. I felt at times like I was being carried along on the tide of excitement and hope, something that seemed quite new to many people in the region. Many of the lads I worked with were ready to roll up the sleeves of their *perple werk sherts* and get Boro *ta'oos on their aaarms*.

The arrival of Nicky Barmby from Spurs in the pre-season did little to dampen the new sense of enthusiasm. This was a young, ambitious player with a bright future who had chosen to leave an apparently more glamorous team. He wasn't just some ageing journeyman looking for a nice cushty pay-day. Boro fans were promised that more players like Barmby would be brought in. The fans just couldn't wait to get into their spanking new stadium and get stuck into the likes of Manchester United and Liverpool.

Teething problems with access to the ground and a delay in obtaining a safety certificate meant a bit of a shuffle with the early fixtures, so Boro had to wait a few days more to play in the (Brought to you by) Cellnet Riverside Stadium. Even the curtain-raising friendly against Sampdoria had to be postponed until well into the season. The first league fixture of the season was against Arsenal at Highbury in a televised match that saw Boro take a deserved lead before being pegged back by the hosts. A 1-1 draw away to the likes of the Gunners was a good, solid start.

The following week, on Saturday 26th August, the waiting was over for Boro fans and for me. While the Boro took to the field and saw off Chelsea with a comfortable 2-0 victory, I found myself getting married at a Methodist church in a small North Yorkshire market town under rainy skies. The previous five or six weeks had seen glorious, sunny weather, but the photographer assured us it would make our photos look better. Shame they didn't reckon with the true Scotsmen amongst the wedding guests. One photo featuring a line of high-kicking kilt-wearing chaps leaves little to the imagination. As for the match, I only found out the result at the reception later, when some friends from work arrived in buoyant mood on a mini-bus. I thought it was just the prospect of free food that cheered them up.

On my return from honeymoon in the Channel Islands (where I'd had to be coaxed and threatened to get on the ancient propeller plane at Manchester Airport), I was invited to attend a match by one of the Senior Surveyors at work, who was a season-ticket holder. I accepted without hesitation and in mid-September I went along to get my first view of the Riverside and saw Boro beat Coventry 2-1. The new stadium was impressive, despite appearing to stick out like a skeletal, white metal thumb in amongst an industrial wasteland of rubble and decaying petrochemical plants. Predictably the media weren't shy in highlighting this juxtaposition when reporting on the club's affairs or when broadcasting the matches on TV. It was to become a sore point with proud Teessiders. As for my match experience, I couldn't fault it. Inside, the stadium was pristine and modern, all painted concrete blocks and white steel holding 30,000 bright red seats around the pristine pitch. The stadium configuration had one large stand-alone main stand (the West Stand) and three smaller stands (North, East, and South) joined together in a horseshoe shape around the other sides of the pitch.

My seat in the lower East Stand provided an excellent view of the action. There wasn't a spare seat to be had, and the atmosphere was electric, even for an all-seater stadium. At half time I looked around me at the beaming faces of Boro fans who had never expected to see themselves in a place like this. The joyous novelty of it all was plain to see on their faces. One man, who was sat a few seats away from me, looked like he wanted to burst with pride, shaking his head as he said to his companion, "This is all ours! I can't believe it, man. This. Is. Ours!" On my way home I bought my first ever edition of the Gazette Sports Pink to read Eric Paylor's take on the match I'd just seen. This was to become something of a Saturday routine for me.

Things continued to get better and better. In October, Boro signed a diminutive young Brazilian player called Osvaldo Giroldo Junior, or Juninho as he was more commonly known. He had featured prominently in a friendly against England at Wembley in the summer and was attracting attention from the likes of Arsenal, so it was seen as a massive coup for Bryan Robson to be able to secure this calibre of player. The town reacted with unbridled joy, stripping sports shops of Brazil football shirts and flags like plagues of massive, bald-headed locusts. Samba bands were hastily thrown together to greet the little midfield wizard, and the excitement reached carnival pitch when he made his debut against Leeds United at the Riverside in early November. It was love at first dribble as the "Little Fella" showed flashes of his devastating turn of pace and incredible ball control. He set up Boro's goal and even managed to get booked after decking a Leeds player twice his size. Skill, pace and the heart of a lion: his place in Boro hearts was cemented from that day forth.

I managed to catch a few more games as the season progressed and if I couldn't go, I endeavoured to watch any matches shown live, or if that wasn't possible, catch highlights on Match of the Day. I persuaded my father to come along again to see a League Cup match against Crystal Palace, and it was on that night I made it clear that I was now a Boro supporter. I bought a red and white scarf bearing the words MIDDLESBROUGH FC from the club shop at the North West corner of the stadium, took it from its carrier bag, and wrapped it around my neck, grinning all the while. My dad wasn't surprised to see this happen, but feigned disappointment that I had apparently switched allegiances from Manchester United. It could have been worse, I said. At least it wasn't Liverpool or Manchester City. I just couldn't help the way it had happened; it just did, and there was no guilt. Manchester United had been a childhood crush, and I had grown. I was starting to settle in this area and this was just a natural, albeit late, development.

The season continued to exceed the Teesside public's wildest dreams, with Liverpool being sent home with their fancy-dan tails between their legs after a 2-1 defeat, and both Manchester City and West Ham being soundly beaten, 4-1 and 4-2 respectively. In the latter months of 1995, Boro moved into the top four of the Premier League. There was many a double-take when people looked at the league table in newspapers around that time, and Boro fans had sore arms from pinching themselves. And the new tattoos.

Reality bit with cold, icy teeth on Boxing Day, as the (I would come to learn) traditional post-Christmas slump took hold, aided and abetted by an injury crisis. Middlesbrough went on a horrible run of a dozen games without a win, including a 5-0 annihilation by Chelsea and home defeats to Newcastle, Everton and Bolton Wanderers. From being a team that was looking likely to qualify for a European competition, they soon sunk to being threatened by relegation. A couple of well-timed wins against Leeds and Sheffield Wednesday saw them rally, however, and Boro managed to finish the season in a creditable twelfth position.

The last day of the season saw the visit of Manchester United, who were crowned Premier League Champions after a thrilling chase to the line with a team who Sky TV seemed to believe were the nation's second-favourite: Newcastle United. The Geordies had been ten or maybe even twelve points ahead at one point, but had caved in under the pressure as a Cantona-inspired United wore them down game by game, sealing the title with a 3-0 win at the Riverside. I don't think too many Boro fans were angry about the home defeat that day, especially as it denied the folk in barcode shirts from up the A19 the title. Keegan's "I will *love it* if we beat them" meltdown on live TV a few weeks earlier had just added to the amusement. Much of the Boro crowd sportingly stayed behind to applaud the newly-crowned Champions. Maybe they even dreamed of seeing that crown-topped trophy back at the Riverside Stadium one day. They had been dreaming of seeing a major trophy for such a long time. Would the Robson Riverside Revolution help make these dreams come true?

Chapter 4 - 1996/97

Four Seasons in One Year

Smiling as the shite comes down... Well, if you don't laugh, you'll probably cry.

1996 was actually quite a tumultuous year in modern history. Looking back through the history books (or Wikipedia as it now known), it looks like the world was starting to go slightly mad. There were wars and conflicts sparking or re-igniting all over the place, with the Middle East and Africa making the most smoke. Osama Bin Laden declared a fatwa, citing the continued US presence in Saudi Arabia and civil war erupted in Chechnya, where the lines between terrorism and rebellion became blurred to many observers. Massacres and bombings weren't the reserve of these regions, however, with horrific shootings occurring in America, Australia and a primary school in a Scottish town called Dunblane. A bomb went off during the Olympic games in Atlanta, Georgia, the IRA bombed Canary Wharf to end their fragile ceasefire, and the aviation industry had a terrible year with planes crashing with indecent regularity.

Cinema-goers seemed to have an appetite for destruction with films like *Independence Day* and *Twister* topping the box-office. The public's music tastes included *Killing Me Softly* by The Fugees, and *Wannabe* by the newly-manufactured, squeaky-clean Spice Girls; a clear sign of emerging insanity if ever there was one.

The world of sport was an interesting and welcome diversion. There were the Olympic Games in Atlanta, of course, and a British driver triumphed in Formula One, with Damon Hill taking the World Championship. In international football, England hosted the European Championships, and the home team - roared on by Skinner and Baddiel's infectious pop anthem – came so close to exorcising the demons of the last forty years, but were once again denied in a penalty shoot-out by the Germans. A certain Gareth Southgate became the latest tear-soaked, penalty-missing fall guy as Andreas Moller struck the winning spot-kick then strutted towards the crowd like a peacock in need of a good slapping.

And then there was the start of THAT season. Boro had enjoyed a reasonably good first season back in the Premier League. To be fair any season that didn't involve a protracted relegation battle was deemed to be a bloody good one given the history of the club. I was seriously considering buying a season ticket myself, and the decision to do so was made simple when Boro announced the signings of Brazilian midfielder Emerson and Juventus's Fabrizio Ravanelli. I heard the news of the latter transfer coup on the radio just as I drove through the gates at the Wilton petrochemical site, where I was now working on secondment at the nylon plant.

It was a stunning story that raised many a brow, and not just on Teesside. A renowned European Cup-winning striker was coming to the Boro. I was shocked, and couldn't imagine how other, longer-term fans must have felt on hearing this news. Hundreds, nay thousands would be choking on their tea-time parmos, no doubt. I was a little disappointed that my boss at the time didn't know about this before it was announced. He had claimed on more than one occasion to have a mate inside the club (or was it a mate of a mate of an uncle of the tea lady?) who would feed him interesting little titbits about the internal machinations of the club.

Ravanelli and Emerson were joined by Danish international striker Mikkel Beck, who signed from German club Fortuna Koln. The anticipation for the new season became unbearable. Everyone at work was buzzing and looking forward to the Boro actually challenging for major honours. No one seemed overly concerned that the team had invested heavily in expensive strikers and in midfield, but hadn't significantly strengthened the defence. Their only signing at the back before the season kicked off was the ageing Brazilian, Branco.

So on a hot and sunny Saturday, 17th August 1996 to be exact, I was picked up by Gaz and his dad (who seemed to be permanently cynical about Boro, even at this time), and we made our way along the busy A66, turning off at the Sainsbury's roundabout to get to the Zetland multi-storey car-park. From there we walked for what felt like ages to get the ground, and took our seats high up in the South East corner of the Riverside stadium, relishing the prospect of seeing a whole season of excitement and maybe even some history being made. The opening fixture was against Liverpool. Everyone knew they were going to give us a good game and hopefully provide some early clues as to how the team were going to fare.

No one was disappointed. The game ebbed and flowed, Liverpool took the lead three times, but Boro fought back to level, earning a 3-3 draw, and the new players showed what we had in store, both good and bad. Ravanelli was the silver-haired star attraction with his debut hat-trick, getting the chance to do his famous shirt-over-head-look-at-this-six-pack-ladies celebration three times. Emerson showed muscular power and elegant poise in the midfield, his enormous mane of hair glistening in the afternoon sun as he put himself about with fearsome strength - I swear I heard the smack up in row 24 as a hapless, weedy Liverpool midfielder bounced off him in one passage of play - before pinging perfect passes out to the wing or up to the front men. Juninho looked even better with quality players round him.

The crowd was in raptures. This was very, very promising, despite the three goals conceded by the somewhat less glamorous players making up the defence. Not to belittle guys like Nigel Pearson and Steve Vickers, of course. They had been key players for the last couple of seasons, but things had stepped up a notch now, or so it was hoped.

The party atmosphere continued as we left the stadium, and I passed a group of men at the Bridge Inn holding post-match pints of lager aloft and singing, to the tune of Dean Martins' *That's Amore*: "*When the White Feather scores, you can hear Boro roar...Ravanelli! When the White Feather scores, you can hear Boro roar...RAVANELLI, show's yer belly!*"

A 1-0 away defeat to Chelsea was followed by a 1-1 draw away to Forest before I got the chance to see the team again, at home to West Ham in early September. I wasn't brave (or wealthy) enough to travel to away games. In that game, and the following midweek fixture against Coventry, Boro played some sparkling football the like of which had possibly never been seen - and rarely seen since - by the team in red and white. Both visiting teams were destroyed by a rampant strike force. Ravanelli and Juninho linked beautifully and even Robbie Mustoe got in on the act with a goal, morphing from midfield journeyman to marauding maestro. If the anticipation had been in orbit before, it was on its way to Alpha friggin' Centauri now.

A 2-1 victory away to Everton featuring another master-class by the Little Fella did little to reduce expectation, and by mid-September, Boro were in the top four of the Premier League again, hoping that this time they could stick around for more than a week or two. Even the media were sitting up and taking notice of these flashy upstarts from the industrial wastelands of the North East. In the meantime, Boro were making quiet progress through the early rounds of the Coca-Cola Cup with consummate ease, slamming in truck-loads of goals against the likes of Hereford and Huddersfield. Even the rarely-playing Branco got in on the goals. Promising wasn't even close: Boro were in dreamland.

I was also in a dreamland of my own, of sorts. I was now living in Teesside with my new wife and had made some good friends. Work was almost enjoyable, even if I did almost soil myself every time the horrendous honking of the test alarm went off at the Nylon plant at Wilton where I was working at the time. There were side benefits, such as taking clients to see matches to the now-fashionable football club in that smoggy town on the Tees. I was part of a group that went to see the league cup match against Huddersfield one midweek night, and we sat in the corporate seats in the West Stand watching Boro give the lower league team a good seeing to. It didn't feel right to be sat there watching a match in a suit and tie, but after a few beers, the ties were loosened along with the tongues and the morals. It was decided that after the match we would sample the delights of a mythical Middlesbrough venue that I had heard people talk of in hushed tones called Club Bongo International. It was located in the mythical region called "over the border", which was presumably inhabited by trolls, orcs and talking trees.

I don't remember a great deal about the nightclub as I had already supped several ales before and during the match, but I remember thinking I had fallen through some time travel vortex into an alternate 1970s. I was surrounded by exotic creatures dressed in leopardskin and smelling like the entire contents of the perfume counter at Debenhams mixed with naughty stuff procured from Amsterdam coffee shops. I left the others to it after an hour, feeling slightly bewildered and lost, but I somehow managed to negotiate my way back to the right side of the border by walking under the ornate, riveted steel structure of the Albert Bridge. As I walked past the thick columns towards where I hoped there would be a taxi to convey me home, a young lady asked me if I was looking for business. I wasn't sure what she meant at first, wondering if she wanted my card, but when I twigged what she was propositioning me with, I picked up my walking pace and left her to try her luck with someone else.

I soon discovered another interesting aspect of living local to Boro: the chance meetings with players. I saw Juninho in a car dealership on Preston Park Industrial Estate, and was too star-struck to wonder why he was looking at Vauxhalls. He nodded at me and said "Hi," whilst I tried my hardest not to swoon like some pale-faced damsel. I also saw Derek Whyte at a petrol station near Yarm, filling his Beamer with petrol and buying expensive sausage rolls, presumably. On the many nights out in Yarm I spent crawling from the Bluebell to the Ketton Ox to the George & Dragon to the Union Arms and finally to the poseurs' palace they call the Black Bull, I would often see players having a few pints. One Saturday night as Neil Cox walked past me, I blurted out, "Good game today, Neil." He looked at me, smiled and replied, "Cheers mate!" My mates ribbed me mercilessly for the rest of the night.

Back to the football, and it's actually quite hard to put a finger on where it started to go wrong. Nigel Pearson suffering a serious injury didn't help matters, particularly in a defence so reliant on his leadership, and teams started to work out our pattern of play and our overreliance on certain players. Arsenal brutally exposed the frailties of the side in our next home game by stifling the creative play in midfield. They left with a 2-0 win and the first cracks started to show. Ravanelli became a frustrated figure, taking out his anger at the linesmen who flagged him offside or at the team-mate who failed to tee him up for a nice, easy tap-in.

For the first time I was getting a sense of what life is really like for long-suffering Boro fan: short bursts of hope followed by long periods of crushing disappointment, the stab to the heart as the away fans cheer another goal, the nausea-inducing sight of them leaping from their seats and punching the air at full-time and the long, tortuous trudge back to the car in the biting docklands wind…

A 4-0 mauling at Southampton was followed by a hard-fought televised 2-2 draw at Roker Park, where Emerson answered the disgusting monkey chants from a section of the home support with one his special net-rippers. The league form had nose-dived and there wasn't another win to celebrate until Boxing Day, when Everton were beaten 4-2 at home with more magic from Juninho.

This didn't seem to worry people too much, however, because the League Cup form was still very good. Newcastle were given a football lesson and beaten 3-1 as Juninho ran them ragged, and Liverpool were sent tumbling out of the competition 2-1. Before we knew it, we were in the League Cup semi-finals, and only - yes, only - Stockport County stood between Middlesbrough and a Wembley final. It had to be written in the stars, right? Not even a dreadful, insipid 2-0 defeat at home to Leicester City made people worry too much.

The next away game, or lack of it, was to become the moment that defined the season. An already injury-affected team was decimated by a virus, leaving squad options for the away game at Blackburn looking terribly limited. If they had managed to pull a team together to play, it would have consisted almost entirely of junior players. Rather than field a team of this nature and face a drubbing, the club management attempted to obtain official dispensation to postpone the fixture, but something went wrong with a fax machine that got clogged up by moustache hairs or something, and the club were left facing sanction from the Premier League for failing to fulfil the fixture. The eventual sanction imposed was a three-point deduction, and this was upheld as being "just and fair" despite an appeal by the club fronted by a top-ranking barrister. Yer jokin' aren't yer?

In the New Year, the season didn't improve much in terms of league results, with abject defeats away to Coventry and Arsenal, as well as a 1-0 reverse at home to Southampton. A 4-2 win against Sheffield Wednesday in mid-January briefly raised our hopes, but they were soon put back in their box after Liverpool destroyed us 5-1 at Anfield. Cheeky chappy touchline-sniffer Robbie Fowler checked his invisible watch after scoring the first within a minute or two of kick off, just to rub it in.

To make matters worse during these dark days, one of our midfield dynamos, Emerson, was playing hide and seek in Brazil and didn't seem to want to come back to these sunny shores, and his wife had apparently described the town as being a "strange and terrible place". It wasn't as if Robbo hadn't tried to accommodate him. He'd taken on his cousin, Fabio, on a trial basis, purportedly to help Emerson settle in. He'd even go on to give the cousin a game in the league cup against some hapless lower-league team who probably thought they were seeing double. Fabio only played once, even though he performed quite well.

Of course the southern-based tabloid media feasted greedily on all of it, making crass comparisons between Rio de Janeiro and Teesside. They had obviously decided that it was high time to stick the boot in on these cheeky upstarts. How dare an unfashionable club from an industrial shit-hole like Middlesbrough try and challenge for honours?

The FA Cup came along as another distraction from the atrocious league form that threatened to pull Boro into a relegation battle that would have seemed ridiculous to most Boro fans only a few months ago. Chester City were given the usual short shrift offered to lower league teams with a 6-1 spanking, and Hednesford showed typical non-league pluck to their huge travelling support but were eventually vanquished. Somehow Boro had conspired to get into the quarter finals, a round they had never got past in their history. Derby County were the next opponents, but we would have to beat them on their patch at the Baseball Ground (their Riverside replica at Pride Park was still under construction at the time).

In February, Boro played Stockport for the honour of playing in the League cup final at Wembley. A 2-0 win in the away leg set up what we thought would be nothing more than a procession for the second leg at home, but we were sadly mistaken once again. Stockport scored a goal to make the crowd tense and uneasy, but Boro managed to hold off the lower division team, and as the fans sang, *"tell your mam, your mam, to put the champagne on ice, we're going to Wembley twice!"* a jittery Boro staggered over the line and into their first major cup final. Belief was still running strong. Even the wretched results in the league and the three-point deduction weren't taking away from this moment. They were in one final and could quite conceivably make a second. Surely they would put 120 years of barrenness behind them this time. Martin O'Neill's Leicester City were to be our opponents in the final.

Back to the reality of the bread and butter of the league and a home loss to Newcastle at the end of February was particularly hard to take. Gaz and I had amused ourselves for a while by laughing at Peter Beardsley's cut-by-his-mum-in-the-bath hairstyle, but for the first time at a Boro match I felt a spiky, menacing atmosphere in the air. On the walk back to the car I passed some scuffles breaking out near the South Stand as the victorious, gloating Geordies exited the stadium. I was beginning to really understand the depth of feeling against the black and white masses from up the A19. I'm sure that the feeling was mutual, despite Geordie protestations that they don't really see us as local rivals.

March saw the league form finally starting to pick up, helped by the recent signings of Italian defensive stallion Gianluca Festa and Aussie shot-stopper Mark Schwarzer, and Boro went on a good run, beating Derby County 6-1 at home - we were never short of goals when in the mood - as well as Blackburn and Chelsea, 2-1 and 1-0 respectively. The latter game featured one of the best Boro goals I have seen live: a diving header by Juninho at the near post after a nice one-two with the much-maligned (especially by Mr Ravanelli) Mikkel Beck. In between these games we stuffed Leicester City at their place, with yet another virtuoso performance by Juninho, who seemed hell-bent on single-handedly keeping Boro in the Premier League.

In hindsight, Juninho might have been better to rein it in a little for that game, because that performance was noticed, not just by Boro fans, but by a certain Martin O'Neill. Another meeting with Derby saw Boro make even more history and progress to the FA Cup semi-final with a 2-1 victory. It was getting hard to keep up with games, and was seriously stretching the pockets of fans, even those who only followed at home.

Time for the League Cup Final, then. It was some weekend. I travelled down to London in a mini-bus with a gang of Gaz's friends on the Saturday afternoon. Another friend called Jeff offered couches and floor space to sleep on at his flat somewhere in North London. We spent a boozy afternoon and night in the capital, falling over more from the price of beer than from the effects of it, culminating in a meet-up in Piccadilly Circus where thousands of Boro fans cavorted in the fountains and clambered over various statues to sing songs about the coming triumph. It was fantastic to be there and witness the atmosphere. Later our group went back to continue the revelry at Jeff's flat in North London, and I have learned since that the noise we made that night almost got Jeff evicted from his flat, thanks to the complaints of the party-pooper, grumpy neighbour downstairs.

Boro had, of course, been to a minor Wembley Final before (if a final can be called minor) in 1990 to play Chelsea in the Zenith Data Systems Cup. They had lost, but that was history now. The League Cup was a proper trophy, contested and won by big teams like Liverpool and Arsenal, even if it came under various names such as

The Milk Cup or The Rumbelows Cup and now under the sponsorship of a world-famous carbonated drink who don't need any advertising in this little book.

The journey up to Wembley on the tube and the game itself are now little more than a haze in my mind. I remember being distinctly underwhelmed by the dilapidated state of Wembley Stadium and far from impressed by the view I had from my seat (actually a plastic bench) that was ten rows or more from the front but still just about level with the pitch. I could just about see the white rectangle of the goal at the far end of the pitch through the perimeter fencing. I'm sure the price of food and drink was a complete disgrace as well, as it invariably is at places such as these. Still, it was good to be there, under the warm April sunshine; my hangover wearing off and hopes running high for the game.

As it was, the game was terrible, judging by the limited action I could see. Juninho – no doubt as a result of the brilliance he displayed against the same opponents a few weeks ago - was man-marked out of the game by an insistent Swedish limpet called Pontus Kaamark and Boro never really got a rhythm going. One wag sitting near me said he'd received news from afar that it was 2-0 midway through the second half, but it wasn't, and the game dragged into extra time.

It was then that it got interesting. Through the fence I saw a goalmouth scramble at the far end of the ground and Ravanelli fired in a rebound (I think) to take us into the lead. The sight of him running with his shirt pulled over his head towards our end was enough to tell us what had happened, and the Boro contingent erupted. I was almost sent tumbling forward a number of rows by people jumping up and down around me. I felt like I'd suddenly arrived at a punk rock concert, and was instantly compelled to join in with the pogo jumping. I had never heard such a noise or seen such movement and colour, as flags and scarves were held aloft and shaken ecstatically. It was truly beautiful and moving. The singing I tried to belt out stuck in my throat with emotion. I had been a Boro fan such a short time, but was so easily carried away by the sheer joy around me.

It wouldn't last, of course. Pesky Emile Heskey bundled the ball over the line in the last minute of extra-time as Bryan Robson dallied over making a substitution, and the mood changed beyond recognition. The noise and flag-waving was now emanating from the opposite end of the ground and the colour was all blue rather than red. That last-minute equaliser probably felt like a win to the Leicester fans; it certainly felt like a crushing defeat to us. I didn't have the heart, let alone the funds, to go to the replay at Hillsborough, which Leicester duly won with a typical long-ball / knock-down Leicester goal from Steve Claridge.

The following weekend a few of the same group that had gone to London drove to Manchester for the FA Cup semi-final against Second Division Chesterfield at Old Trafford. Boro were red-hot favourites to reach their second cup final of the season, but things were never going to run that smoothly. Oh no. The cup always throws up surprises, and we were nearly another victim of a giant-killing.

For just a moment I felt strange sitting there in the huge main stand of Old Trafford and supporting Boro, stranger still to watch the Chesterfield fans, most of whom were probably at the only game they'd ever been to in their life, trying to goad Boro fans with oh-so-original chants of, *"going down, going down, going down!"* I laughed it off as a bit of small-club mentality, but I wasn't laughing when Chesterfield raced into a 2-0 lead. Boro seemed to freeze in the spotlight, and worse was to come as Vladimir Kinder got red-carded for fouling the young Kevin Davies (he'll be back to bother Boro again, I bet). It was looking pretty grim, but somehow, our team dug deep, rolled their sleeves up and dragged us back into the game.

We survived a horrible moment when the referee, David Elleray, decided to deny the "Spireites" what looked like a perfectly legitimate goal. That marked a turning point and Boro took charge of the game, going into a 3-2 lead in extra time with a Festa goal. We felt sure we'd be going to Wembley again, but for the second week running, there was to be a late twist and Chesterfield snatched a last-minute equaliser as some player whose name I forget headed in a long, raking cross. I left the stadium feeling numb. Surely this couldn't be happening; not again. But it bloody well was, you know.

Another replay at Hillsborough, then, and we saw off Chesterfield 3-0 in the end, but the league fixtures were now piling up in a backlog thanks to these cup runs. In April, there was a flurry of games, but the form dipped again just when wins were sorely needed. A rain-sodden game on May Day Bank Holiday Monday at Old Trafford saw Boro leading Manchester United 3-1 with some absolutely stunning play that had even Manchester United fans applauding, but we were pegged back to 3-3. There was a frustrating 0-0 with Blackburn in the re-arranged, apparently illegally-postponed fixture, a 1-1 draw with fellow strugglers Nottingham Forest, and another horrible local derby against Sunderland, which ended 1-0 to the jammy Mackems.

In the last home game of the season we played Aston Villa, needing a win to have any chance of staying up. I needed to leave early to drive up to a family gathering in Scotland, and had to pull myself away from a nail-biting game that was poised at 2-2 as I left the stadium. I missed Ravanelli's dramatic late winner from the penalty spot, but heard the cheers coming from the stadium as I approached the A66 underpass. The victory was confirmed when I got to my car and tuned in to the radio commentary.

It all came down to the last league game of the season. We still had a chance, but would have to beat Leeds United at Elland Road, and that was not going to be easy. Leeds were another club with which there was no love lost, given the Yorkshire connection (oh no, don't say Middlesbrough is in Yorkshire, that's asking for a 200-post internet debate), so they weren't likely to do us any favours. Coventry, Sunderland and Forest were also in the danger zone, but our fate was squarely in our own hands.

I watched the game live on Sky Sports. It was nerve-wracking, gut-wrenching and everything else that you'd come to expect from a relegation decider. Given the circumstances, Boro played OK, and even managed to come back from 1-0 down to draw level, (Brian bloody Deane scored against us again, as he seemed to do every time he played against us) but we just couldn't find the crucial winning goal that would have saved us. Beck missed a late sitter from a Juninho pass, and our fate was sealed. The season that had started so well and with so much potential had ended with the awful reality of relegation back to Football League Division One, along with Nottingham Forest and Sunderland.

I was devastated, and the players looked shell-shocked on my TV screen. Juninho sat on the turf, his head bowed and in tears; a small, dejected figure oblivious to the sickening *schadenfreude* raining down from the home fans. It was well-known that he would probably be on his way to another club now, and all I could think of was what could have been. We could and should have survived and could have signed even more world-class players in during the summer. We could and probably should have played that Blackburn game, got heavily beaten, and still survived. If only Heskey hadn't scored in the Coca-Cola Cup Final, because I'm convinced that took the wind out of our sails for the rest of the season....so many ifs and ands and pots and pans...but no glory. It was my first genuine taste of this kind of pain, but I'm sure it doesn't get any easier however many times it happens.

The FA Cup Final was a waste of time, in the end. I travelled by coach this time, down and back on the same day this time, unable to afford another weekend on the lash in London. Even if I could have afforded it, my wife of just short of two years may not have appreciated it.

At the stadium I sat in my seat and tried to enjoy the Cup Final atmosphere with the military band and the singing of "Abide With Me", but it all felt a little flat, to be honest. Boro fans roused themselves to make their point about the deduction of the three points to the FA dignitaries as they dragged their suited carcasses away from their comfy executive seats onto the pitch to meet the players. Later on the radio, some pompous, clueless arse called David Mellor tried to make out we had been chanting, "Sieg Heil," rather than, "Three Points."

The game itself was over after forty-odd seconds when Roberto Di Matteo was given the freedom of London to pick his spot from thirty yards and launch the ball over the despairing dive of Ben Roberts and into the net. A perfectly good Festa goal was disallowed for offside and this only served to irritate as Chelsea went on to win 2-0 and take the cup. It wasn't really a surprise. The coach journey home was long and quiet, punctuated by freakish lightning storms on the M1.

There was an open-top bus parade through the town centre a week after the cup final. It obviously wasn't a victory parade, more a thank you to fans. The crowds came along and waved at their fallen heroes, wondering if they'd ever see the likes of Ravanelli and Emerson again, and wondering where Juninho was. I hoped it was just that he couldn't bear the thought of saying good-bye to the fans he had made such a connection with. He was a top-level player who deserved to play on the biggest stages, and was soon on his way to play for Atletico Madrid.

So that was the season that was, and enough happened to fill four seasons. The dream that had begun with a bang ended with a nightmarish whimper, like the last bit of air coming out of a balloon. Boro had to face the next season in the second tier and would probably face it without most of the great players they had bought.

What hurt most about it all was the sense of injustice over the three-point fiasco. We felt that our little club had been singled out and made an example of. Whilst there was great sadness, lurking beneath there was a feeling that we had to roll our sleeves up, dust ourselves down and bounce back. Boro had come back from the dead in '86, hadn't they?

As for me... well I wasn't put off supporting them in the slightest. There was no way I was giving up on them. I was still in the honeymoon period, even if I was married to a rollercoaster addict.

Chapter 5 - 1997/98

Bouncebackibility

Let's take a big breath and start again, shall we? We needed to after that last season, not to mention that year. It was memorable, alright…memorable in a win-a-grand-on-a-scratch-card-and-drop-it-down-a-drain-on-your-way-to-collect-the-winnings way.

What do you do after that? You go and buy another scratch card, that's what you do. I renewed my season ticket, and the wife decided she wanted to come along and watch too, having tasted the live experience of a game the previous season when I took her along to a league cup match. She obviously decided I was spending too many hours at football matches…without her. We'd only been married for two years so we were still comfortable spending a lot of time together. Young love…*sigh*

On a personal level, 1997 was a pretty good year. We had a fantastic two-week camping holiday in France, with one week in Gironde and the other in the Dordogne. It rained quite a bit but the food and wine made up for it. In the spring I finally finished my five-year day-release degree at Newcastle and a month or two later got the news that I'd passed with a Desmond (2.2). My stock was steadily rising at work, and the future was looking good.

In the wider world things weren't as turbulent as in 1996, but there were still some massively pivotal events. Tony Blair's New Labour crew stormed the general election on 1st May, promising a change from the old ways and a final goodbye to eighteen long years of Tory rule. Things could only get better, they told us. I don't think I'll ever recover from the sight of a dancing John Prescott.

At the end of August, Britain changed beyond recognition with the sudden death of Diana, Princess of Wales, Queen of Hearts, English Rose, and so on. I heard the news when the radio alarm clock woke me later that morning. I thought it was the Queen Mother at first with all the talk of a royal death, but when it became clear who had actually met their demise, it was quite a shock. The aftermath was unbelievable. It doesn't really need dwelling on in this medium; suffice to say it made mawkish, cosmetic displays of public grief acceptable in a country famous for keeping control of one's emotion and not making a scene, with perhaps a slightly trembling lip. I've even had staff in foreign hotels telling me that my country is not the same now following her death. What do you say to that? Agree, perhaps, and weep gently on their shoulder.

In cultural terms, it was a bit of a lean year. James Cameron's sea-sickly blockbuster *Titanic* broke box-office records, and George Lucas gave us unnecessary remixes of the perfect *Star Wars* Trilogy. In music Puff Daddy and Aqua dominated the charts, but both lagged well behind Elton John's tribute to Diana, *Candle in the Wind*. The whole world was going soft in the head.

But back to the really important stuff: the game of football. The new season was actually quite keenly anticipated, despite the fact Boro were back in the lower division. Season tickets were selling well and full houses were almost guaranteed for every home game. My wife and I went to see the razzmatazz-fuelled release of the new season's kits at the stadium and duly bought one shirt each. Her indoors got the home one featuring the white chest band, which was back after a long absence (since the '70s, I believe). I got the away shirt, which was a blue number with a wide white Y down the front. Both had BORO emblazoned on the back at the bottom. We must have looked a right pair of berks wearing them, to be honest.

The season tickets – those red, wallet-sized, plastic booklets – duly arrived in the post and it was pleasing to note that they were thicker than last season. Lower league football is better value, you see; more games for your money. The fact that the games were against the likes of Crewe Alexandra and Tranmere Rovers rather than Manchester United and Liverpool was neither here nor there....honest.

At the beginning of the season we had managed to hold onto Ravavelli and Emerson somehow, or maybe they hadn't managed to get away yet. Either way, there was still quality in the side. The addition of Paul Merson from Arsenal was a really, really good bit of business by Bryan Robson and the board. In midfield we added experience and nous in the form of Andy Townsend and in defence we still had the slightly unhinged but ever-popular Festa and the solid presence of Mark Schwarzer. We felt confident that we could get back into the top flight straight away.

The opening day against Charlton was a strange one. It finally hit home where we actually were, and the team struggled and toiled to come back from a goal down and beat the South London team 2-1, with Ravanelli heading the late winner. I had the feeling we'd have a few games like this, where we had to scrap for the points. It wasn't all going to be pretty, flowing football. We lost the next game at home to Stoke in a turgid 1-0 defeat thanks to a goal by a man who looked like my old boarding school matron, Paul Stewart, and the pre-season optimism was melting faster than a snowman on holiday in the Sahara desert.

Things improved once the obviously-disruptive element known as the White Feather left the club. He finally managed to buy his ticket out of town and, in truth, we weren't sad to see him go in the end. His bad-mouthing of the club added to his on-pitch histrionics had started to irritate a significant proportion of the faithful. With his souring influence gone, the team went on a good run through to the end of September, culminating in a famous, televised 2-1 victory over the Mackems at their new Stadium of Light. Emerson was once more their tormentor, spanking home a stunning volley to once again silence the knuckle-dragging monkey chants (ironic, huh?). Merson showed the finesse and vision we would come to rely on, setting up the winner for the ever-reliable Robbie Mustoe.

A home defeat to Sheffield United was ultimately just a blip as Boro steadied the early-season wobbles and started to climb the table. They also started on another cup run in the Coca-Cola cup, quietly seeing off Barnet over two legs before beating Sunderland again and defeating Bolton. No one really expected us to go much further than that, to be fair. This season the priority was promotion.

An away defeat to Wolves in early November was followed by an eight-game unbeaten run. Mikkel Beck, now free of the hectoring of a certain grey-haired Italian started banging in the goals, and Merson also managed to locate his scoring boots. Around that time construction works commenced in the empty corners of the ground, which would eventually add another 5,000 to the capacity for the start of next season. The club was confident they could get back into the elite league and fill these extra seats.

With Christmas approaching Boro were at the business end of the table, challenging for automatic promotion. Two away defeats (to

Manchester City and Charlton) either side of the silly season slowed the momentum down a touch, but February saw a fine sequence of results, with five out of six league games won and the other drawn. Even the inevitable departure of Emerson following more of his jolly AWOL japes didn't affect the team.

The New Year also saw the visit of Arsenal to the Riverside for the 3rd round FA Cup tie. Despite Merson scoring against his old team (and rushing to the North Stand to emphatically kiss the club badge on his shirt) Arsenal won 2-1 and knocked us out.

February wasn't just good because of the league results. Something special and quite unexpected was happening in another competition. In the Coca-Cola cup Boro had beaten Reading 1-0 away in the quarter finals and suddenly found themselves one round away from another Wembley final. All that stood between them was a team called Liverpool. "It had been a good run", was the natural thought that popped into my mind when I heard that draw. With some developments at work, I wasn't going to be too bothered if they got knocked out because I would probably miss seeing the final. Selfish, I know. So sue my ass. I wouldn't even get to see it on TV where they were thinking of sending me...to Minneapolis in the United States of America.

As it turned out, the first leg at Anfield was a tight affair and Boro took the lead when Townsend sent Merson clear, but we eventually lost 2-1. No one really expected us to triumph after that. We were just a lowly First Division team and had to win by two clear goals. Still, the club announced that the second leg would be a "Flag Day", encouraging the fans to bring scarves, flags and all manner of noisy things with them and create as much noise and colour as possible. The club were bang on the money with the initiative they showed and the atmosphere was incredible that night, arguably the best it has ever been at the Riverside. Even Mark Page was caught up in the buzz, putting aside his usual clumsy, cack-handed attempts at atmosphere-creation and helping to get the capacity crowd going with stirring pieces of classical music. There was just something in the air that night.

It must have carried to the dressing room. Boro came out and found themselves with a 2-0 lead within a few minutes. A Merson penalty and a goal from debutant veteran striker Marco Branca, fresh off the plane from Italy, put the fans into a state of utter delirium. All we had to do now was hold out for the remaining eighty-five minutes plus stoppage time. A young full-back called Steve Baker gave the performance of his life to man-mark the dangerous Steve McManaman out of the game and Liverpool just couldn't get any rhythm going. Boro played like the lions on their shirts, roared on by the joyous noise from the stands, and pulled off an amazing, unexpected victory to get back to Wembley.

Some of that special atmosphere echoed into the weekend with Boro putting the Mackems to the sword for the third time that season. Branca scored twice this time and another new signing, the young and promising floppy-fringed Alun Armstrong, got on the score sheet in a 3-1 win. It was all going swimmingly. Automatic promotion was within reach and another cup final beckoned.

It was around then that matters at work suddenly came to a head and I was told that I was needed in the USA. I just couldn't turn such an opportunity down. I had never been outside Europe and now my job was giving me the chance to see the big wide world. I had to accept. I wasn't sure how long I'd be going for, but it had the potential to turn into a long-term move, although I would be going alone to start with.

Out of the blue, Boro's fortunes took a sudden, unexpected nose-dive. A 4-0 battering away to fellow promotion contenders Nottingham Forest was followed by an abject 5-0 humiliation at QPR, featuring the infamous antics of on-loan 'keeper, Andy Dibble. We were slipping, and our goal difference suffered somewhat, courtesy of nine goals conceded without reply. We went into the next home game against Swindon needing to score six to go back to the top. And, as it happened, this would also be my last game before I travelled to America.

The six goals duly came. Branca, Armstrong and Neil "Mad House" Maddison got a brace apiece, with Maddison scoring from a quite stunning long-range volley from the edge of the area. That was a goal of the season contender itself, but not to be outdone, Branca scored with a beauty of an overhead bicycle kick just as full time was approaching, and Boro stormed back to the top of Division One.

It was a superb way for me to leave them, and a few days later I bade a tearful goodbye to my wife and parents at Teesside airport and started the long journey to the American Mid-West, which started with a short hop in a little Fokker to Amsterdam. On the second leg, as the KLM jumbo flew over the Christmas cake landscapes of Greenland, I looked pensively out of the window, listening to The Verve's *Urban Hymns* on a constant loop on my portable CD player. *Bittersweet Symphony* couldn't have been any more apt.

My view of the remaining few games of the season was somewhat patchy and almost completely masked by the many miles between Minneapolis and Middlesbrough. I had to rely on my wife to relay the scores when I spoke to her on the phone (although I always asked her how she was first, to be polite) or tune in to the BBC's World Service for Sports Report on the cheap short-wave portable radio I bought in a branch of Radio Shack. There was no broadband internet those days and no world-wide wall-to-wall TV coverage of English Premier League football, let alone mention of the lower leagues. I was surrounded by people whose idea of sport was spending three hours plastered in body paint watching blokes in tights and shoulder-pads running on and off a field covered in lines and numbers, and sometimes they might even throw the ball. Or there was baseball, which was probably as inscrutable to me as cricket is to an American.

Never mind. I still managed to follow the results. Boro - or Typical Boro, as I was now starting to call them after a just couple of seasons of following them – seemed to be doing their best to avoid automatic promotion and apparently wanted to take their chances in the lottery of the play-offs. At the start of April we lost two consecutive away games to West Brom and Sheffield United (the latter one of those teams I was learning is a bogey team) and things weren't looking too clever. Somewhere around that time Boro signed another couple of players: a Colombian chap called Hamilton Ricard and a Geordie called Paul Gascoigne. You may have heard of him. It was hoped these two new recruits would help Boro in their final push for promotion.

Then came the League Cup final, which this season was against Chelsea. Chelsea, Chelsea, Chelsea. They seem to have a habit of standing in Boro's way at Wembley. They had beaten us in the ZDS final in 1990 and in the FA Cup last term, and here they were again: brazen, blue, cockney sparras, trying to play with the big boys in the top flight. Who did they think they were? You can't take anyone seriously when Santa Claus is in charge. Dennis Wise was the chief elf, presumably.

My wife and sister-in-law got tickets and went down on a coach to see the game, but my experience of the final was via my little radio. I'd hoped that they might carry the whole game, but instead concentrated on a couple of Premier League games that were on at the same time with the odd report from Wembley. It was 0-0 at full time and so went into extra-time. We still had a chance, then, and here I was, 4,000 miles away, listening to a crackly radio that only gave me occasional snippets of the action. I should have been there, witnessing what could have been the biggest day in Boro's history. Damn my ambition. Damn my nomadic spirit.

Then came the news that there had been a goal. They didn't say which team had scored, but instead played a replay of the commentary starting just before the goal. This was obviously designed to ramp up the tension for Boro and Chelsea fans like me around the globe, huddling close to their wireless sets.

"Gascoigne with the ball in midfield," said the commentator. "It's a Boro goal," thought I, "it has to be if we've got the ball!"

Wrong. Gazza lost the ball and before I knew it Chelsea were in the lead. I can't remember who scored, someone instantly forgettable like Eddie Newton perhaps; it doesn't really matter. The game was up. Chelsea scored a second soon after and I switched off my radio. I had been considering hunting down the off-chance of a delayed relay of the game in some sports bar somewhere down town, but decided I couldn't face it. There was no point now. I consoled myself with a Chinese takeaway from the restaurant round the corner from my apartment. The restaurant was called Robert Lee's. I'm sure it wasn't actually named after a Newcastle midfielder who had allegedly been convinced by Keegan that Newcastle is closer to London than Middlesbrough is, but hey, give me a break.

My next big meeting with the radio was on 3rd May: the final day of the season. Boro had strung together a good run to keep themselves in contention, with three 1-0 wins against Reading, Man City and Port Vale followed by a 1-1 draw with Wolves leading up to the last game at home to Oxford United. Nottingham Forest were already up and it was between ourselves and Sunderland for the second automatic spot. We had to win to be sure.

I existed in a somewhat agitated, unknowing state all morning until I was able to get the result on the radio. The final scores came through and I waited patiently, imagining every possibility, every permutation. For me they all existed simultaneously, like some quantum physics experiment featuring an irritated cat in a box. Finally, I was put out of my misery. Middlesbrough 4, Oxford United 1. We were up. Get in.

My stay in America didn't last long. I was offered a long-term position but for various reasons – including my wife's reluctance to move there – I decided to return to the North East of England. In my last few weeks state-side I was able to see Arsenal secure the double by beating the Geordies in the FA Cup Final and a couple of the opening games of the '98 World Cup on a large screen in a British pub that I had come to call my second home in Minneapolis. The American commentators on the US channels were clueless, but that didn't matter. I was amongst fellow Englishmen, watching football games, singing songs, drinking beer and it felt good, even if the games started at 9am local time.

Either way, I was on my way home. I couldn't miss out on Boro's return to the Premier League, could I now?

Chapter 6 - 1998/99

Back Where We Belong

No one would have believed that in the last years of the 20th Century, Boro's affairs were being watched by full houses at the Riverside Stadium.

But it's true; they were.

In the wider world of 1998, we saw India and Pakistan enter the nuclear arms race with a series of alarming bomb tests. Bill Clinton defended himself against Monica Lewinsky's accusations of sexual deviancy, whilst a certain Saudi called Osama Bin Laden became more and more infamous with his name being linked the US embassy bombings in Kenya and Tanzania. A firm called Google began operations and Sky TV started their digital service. Old Blue Eyes, Frank Sinatra, joined the heavenly choir...

In the box office, Speilberg's epic war film, *Saving Private Ryan*, was top-grosser, and *Armageddon* and *Deep Impact* showed an end-of-millennium appetite for global annihilation.

In the world of music, large-nosed North American women dominated the popular charts, with Celine Dion and Cher having the best-selling singles of the year. The album charts were full of old rockers like The Rolling Stones, Eric Clapton and Jimmy Page and there were Greatest Hits compilations galore from the likes of Depeche Mode and U2. Nostalgia ain't what it used to be.

In football's World Cup, France took the trophy, beating a subdued Brazil in the final in Paris. In other sporting arenas, Mika Hakkinen took the F1 Championship and France won the Five Nations Rugby tournament with a Grand Slam.

I returned to the UK in late June, around four months after leaving for the USA. I arrived home just in time to catch the England v Argentina match in the second round of the World Cup. I'm sure we all remember Michael Owen's wonder goal, Beckham's sending off, Shearer's elbow leading to Campbell's golden goal being disallowed and the inevitable penalty shoot-out defeat. This manner of elimination from major tournaments was becoming a habit.

At least Boro gave us something to cheer with their promotion back to the Premier League, joined by Nottingham Forest and Charlton Athletic. The latter team had beaten Sunderland in the play-off final, much to the amusement of Boro and Newcastle fans. Those newly-filled in corners would be complete for the start of the new season as well.

All kinds of rumours were heard over the weeks leading up to the season. I even heard someone at work talking about Gabriel Batistuta coming to the club. That would have been some coup, but I was soon to learn how to deal with any rumours I heard…i.e. ignore them until you hear the announcement of the signing on the news or read it in the paper…then again, that depends which paper. Our only additions pre-season were a couple of defensive ones, in the shape of Dean Gordon and Colin Cooper, one of the heroes of 1986, returning to the club after a long spell at Nottingham Forest.

Despite the lack of headline-grabbing signings, the excitement was palpable on the opening day of the season with a game home against Leeds United. My wife and I resumed our matchday routine: parking at the Zetland multi-storey car park, walking past the station, turning left at the Cornerhouse pub, crossing the road under Albert Bridge and then turning right up Bridge Street before striking out across the bleak, post-apocalyptic, development-free landscape on the approach to the stadium.

We entered the ground near the South East corner and took our seats well before kick-off, getting a good view of the new shape and feel of the stadium with those newly filled-in corners. It looked slightly strange at first due to the transition from the West stand to the corners; it looked as if two stadiums of slightly different sizes had been welded together. It was still impressive, though. Once the ground was full of supporters the little niggles were forgotten and we got on with the business of drawing with Leeds again. It was an uninspiring start to the season, and it wasn't going to get much better in the next few games. A limp 3-1 defeat away to Villa was followed by a 1-1 draw at home to Derby. All very frustrating.

Then there was the sudden departure of Paul Merson. He made some quite remarkable allegations in the press about the drinking and gambling culture at the club, and said this brought back worries he had following his own battles with addiction. The inevitable inquiries began: was there really such a culture at the club? What had Gazza done this time? After being one of the key players in the promotion campaign, Merson was now a pariah to many fans. The badge-kissing act he had performed after scoring against Arsenal in the FA Cup last season was now a distant memory. On the bright side, it was seen as a good bit of business when Boro received a nice big transfer fee from Aston Villa for the want-away player.

The striker situation suddenly didn't look as good as it did last season. In addition to Merson's departure, Marco Branca had departed and Alun Armstrong suffered a long-term injury that would see him out for the majority of the season.

In the meantime I was getting frustrated at work. On my return from the US, my company had decided to send me back on to a chemical plant at Wilton, maybe to serve some kind of penance for upsetting the boss of the American arm of the firm. It was a maintenance project, and involved measuring pipe lagging and scaffolding. All very frustrating, uninspiring and tedious. I didn't even have the internet to while away the hours on in those days, and spent my time drawing abstract art on my computer's paint program and polishing up my CV. I had a few weeks of overlap with another chap from my company but he soon left me alone and I felt somewhat isolated. There was a popular saying in my company: Out on site, out of mind. I was a bum on a seat earning a fee, and that's all that mattered.

Back to the football, and Boro suddenly started winning. They beat Leicester 1-0 and Spurs 3-0, both away from home. Ham the Man Ricard was getting the measure of Premiership defences. A 2-2 home draw with Everton followed. We just couldn't win at home.

Chelsea beat us 2-0 at Stamford Bridge and then we were back at home, facing Sheffield Wednesday. This time we found our pattern, and stuffed them 4-0. Beck got a brace, with Ricard and Gazza grabbing the other goals. Two weeks later Blackburn Rovers were the visitors and were sent home defeated after a late goal by the evergreen Curtis Fleming. His goals are about as frequent as an appearance of Halley's Comet, so he celebrated this one with some enthusiasm.

The next four games were draws. We were turning into the draw specialists. Brian Deane, a Boro tormentor of times gone past, joined the club in late October, making a scoring debut against fellow promoted team, Nottingham Forest. He wasn't anywhere near the Merson mould of course, and fans wondered which direction Bryan Robson was heading in terms of tactics. Was he going for a more direct approach with the big bustling striker?

The next game was thoroughly bizarre affair at Southampton followed, which saw us coming back late in the game to salvage a 3-3 draw. It was one of those games that had everything…apart from a dog on the pitch.

Dean Gordon scored his first goal against Coventry in the next home game, which was a 2-0 win, and then Brian Deane again showed his ability to be a complete pain in the arse to opposing defences by helping us gain a creditable 1-1 draw at Highbury. Then we had the Geordies at home. It was a midweek evening game on a chilly December night and it ended 2-2, but we really should have won. A couple of our veteran players grabbed the goals, in the form of Townsend and Cooper, and Gazza was accosted on the pitch by some festive-spirited and under-dressed ladies who were visibly feeling the cold.

I remember this game for more than just the football, because the next day I met Mark Schwarzer at Harrogate railway station. (I was on my way to London for an interview, having decided I couldn't bear the ICI Wilton isolation treatment any more). It was a few minutes before I was certain who I was stood next to on the platform, and I tried not to sound like a complete fool when I spoke to him. My opening gambit of, "Those Geordies were lucky last night," caught him by surprise, I think. "Yeah, mate, they were," he replied, and said that he wasn't often recognised in Harrogate. We had a little chat and then the train arrived. I resisted the temptation to sit opposite him and stare at him all the way to Leeds.

A 1-0 win at home to the Hammers was followed by a famous day for the Boro. On the 10th December we travelled to Old Trafford to play Manchester United, expecting a bit of a lesson in football at the very least. Bernie Slaven, legend of the Holgate End fence, was commentating on the game for local radio and made a rather rash prediction that we wouldn't get anything from the game. He said that if we won he would bare his backside in the window of the Binn's department store in Middlesbrough town centre. He should have kept quiet, because Ricard, Deane and Gordon put us into a 3-0 lead. United could only get back two of the goals and we hung on for a marvelous victory. I even rang my dad afterwards to have a bit of a gloat. It was such a rare occurrence that I was sure he wouldn't hold it against me for too long.

Good old Bernie was true to his word and carried out his threat, wearing a kilt and having the numbers 3 and 2 written on his buttocks to show to the waiting public and local press. Boro's mascot, Roary the lion, was there as well and seemed to find it all very amusing. Lions in football kits can laugh at what they like, to be fair.

And then it was Christmas. On the last day of work before the break I left my job with the Stockton firm after an eight-year stint, striking out on my own as a freelancer. I didn't even get a card or a present from work (they'd probably forgotten I existed after sending me to site), so I decided to take a huge bottle of Bell's whisky from the office party in lieu.

In Yarm later that afternoon, in my state of emotional inebriation, I almost managed to get our group chucked out of one of the pubs because I wasn't very subtle about drinking out of the enormous bottle I still had with me. I got home in rather a state and managed to spill the cup coffee my wife made for me. I then read a newsletter from my old senior school that had arrived that day, and found out that an old classmate had recently committed suicide. I sat on the stairs, drunk as a skunk, crying into the newsletter and saying this poor fellow's name over and over again. Life…it's a funny old game.

I started a freelance position in London just after the New Year, and spent the next four months travelling down to The Smoke on a Sunday night and returning on a Friday afternoon. It wasn't an ideal situation, but I still managed to get to the Saturday home games.

Boro's fortunes went rapidly down the swanny at that point, as they invariably seem to do after every Christmas. We went all the way to mid-March without a win, losing to Derby, Leeds, Sheffield Wednesday, Liverpool (twice) and Everton as well as going out in the third round of the FA Cup 3-1 to Manchester United. It was a run of seven defeats and three draws, with only five goals scored and twenty-one conceded. If it hadn't been for the early-season good form, relegation might have been a real worry. There weren't even any cup runs to warm the cockles this season, as we had also been knocked out of the League Cup in the third round.

At one night match – I can't remember which one exactly – we were sat in front of a lady and her young, curly-haired child. The child was about eight years old at most, and had that inherent inability to sit still for any length of time, and so proceeded to kick the back of my wife's chair throughout the game. My wife became increasingly annoyed at this, and kept looking at me then looking behind her at said child. Midway through the second half I turned round and asked the child politely to please stop kicking the chair before turning back to watch the game.

Only a few minutes later I heard the sound of gentle sobbing coming from behind me. I turned and saw that the child was burying its curly-haired head into its mother's shoulder, and the mother was doing the best job of soothing that she could. I felt utterly rotten, and at the end of the match, as we made our way to the exits, I apologised to the lady for upsetting her son. As if I hadn't felt bad enough already, she then informed me that the child was in fact a girl. I quickly grabbed my wife's arm and we skulked off as fast as we could into the night feeling terrible and dreading the appearance of the little girl's father at the next match. If he did come, he didn't say anything. I think they realised I meant no harm, even if my gender identification abilities were a bit off.

Back in the world of Boro's season a seven-game unbeaten run started in mid-March with a 3-0 win against Sheffield Wednesday, followed by wins against Nottingham Forest, Wimbledon, Charlton and Coventry, and draws against Blackburn and Chelsea away. We were hovering in the upper-middle regions of the table, and knew that if it hadn't been for that bad run, we could have been challenging for a European spot. How fickle our fortunes, and indeed our feelings, could be.

Of course, the fact that we were safe from relegation by early April should have been something to be proud of. The other promoted teams were struggling badly, battling with Blackburn Rovers (Premier League champions only four years ago) and a few other perennial strugglers for survival.

The season was petering out and there wasn't much to play for now. Arsenal visited the Riverside in late April and gave one of the best displays of attacking football by an away team that I have ever witnessed. We were torn to pieces that day, with the Nigerian Kanu giving us a master-class in outrageous skill and finishing. The flicked back-heel goal from the edge of the penalty area was just ridiculous, and almost everyone in the stadium applauded it. I left at 6-0, having seen enough. Alun Armstrong scored a consolation goal towards the end to sarcastic cheers and renditions of "pig bag" by the visiting fans. You'd think Mark Page would have realized that this piece of music has potential for infinite mockery, but it was still used in 2010. Ho hum.

Into May, then, and I managed to blag myself a job closer to home in Leeds. The commute from Ingleby Barwick wasn't much fun, but at least I was home every night. The last three games of the season saw a 1-1 draw with Newcastle at their place followed by a 1-0 home defeat to Manchester United. They, of course, were on their way to an historic treble of Premier League, FA Cup and UEFA Champions League, culminating in that dramatic injury-time comeback against Bayern Munich in Barcelona. Our last game was a meaningless 4-0 defeat away to West Ham, and the season was over. We finished ninth, and were only six points off our last opponents, who ended the season in fifth position. All those draws (fifteen of them) and that terrible run had put paid to what could have been a superb season. We couldn't complain too much, of course. In our first season back up we finished in the top half and were four places above Newcastle.

I'd take that at the start of any season, thank you very much.

Chapter 7 - 1999/00

We're gonna party like it's...

MCMXCIX. End of the world? Not on your Nelly, unless you think the establishment of the Euro zone qualifies as Armageddon. In other world news this year it kicked off in Kosovo, the Scottish Parliament opened, the world's population reached the six billion mark (it had been just shy of four billion when I was born) and there was yet another infamous massacre in the US, this time at Columbine High School. The millennium computer bug failed to put in an appearance, despite the tabloid running typically hysterical scare stories of planes falling out of the sky and people's porn collections being wiped off hard disks all over the globe.

The world of film offered a mixed bag, with *Star Wars Episode I: The Phantom Menace* grossing stupid amounts of money before word got out that it was actually pretty shite (damn you George Lucas, weeing all over my childhood memories like that!). *The Sixth Sense, Toy Story 2* and *The Matrix* were also major blockbusters, and Sam Mendez's seminal *American Beauty* showed the world what happens to middle-aged bald men trapped in suburban hell.

In music, a young nymph called Britney urged the world to assault her just once more, TLC sang about medical work-wear, Lou Bega went straight to *Mambo No. 5* and Bloodhound Gang had a case of *Bad Touch*. In non-football sport, the Denver Broncos retained the Super Bowl, the first man on the moon won his first Tour de France, Mika Hakkinen won the F1 championship (again) and Australia took the egg-chasing World Cup. Oh, and in tennis Andre Agassi won the French and US opens.

But who really cares about other sport? It's there to put on the telly and annoy the wife with when the football's not on, I suppose. Boro were looking forward to another season in the top flight after coming in a very promising ninth place last time round. A number of major signings in the form of Paul Ince, Christian Ziege and the return of Gary Pallister from Manchester United increased the Teesside public's anticipation. No, we will never, ever learn.

The season started at home to Bradford City, on the ridiculously early date of 7th August. Boro were obviously still on holiday and lost

1-0 to the Premiership new boys from West Yorkshire. A visit to the potentially pugilistic Wimbledon was next up in the midweek game, but Boro managed a 3-2 win with Ham the man scoring twice and the new German full-back getting his first for the club.

I remember the day after that match quite vividly. I had the day off to take my wife to South Tees Hospital for an operation in the morning and came home to wait for the call to pick her up. As I waited I witnessed the total solar eclipse from my back garden, looking up through a partly-cloudy sky to see the sun being slowly devoured by the shadow of the moon. The peculiar half-light that descended combined with an eerie quietness that had me wondering if Nostradamus was onto something when he wrote about the "Great King of Terror" coming from the sky. But of course the sun returned to the sky and we're all still here eleven years later, waiting for the next "end of the world" to come along sometime in 2012.

The world kept on going then, and Boro saw off Derby in their new Riverside-clone stadium. Ricard and Ziege once again scored, along with Brian Deane for a comfortable 3-1 victory. Was this a good run being put together?

It was Liverpool at home the following weekend, and big Brian scored the only goal for a 1-0 win. Oh no...hope was *definitely* rising once more. Three wins on the bounce and we were right up there in the mix, even though it was really, really early days. Any Boro fan will tell you how good it feels to read the papers or Ceefax and see the name of Middlesbrough near the top of the Premier League table, even after only four games.

We had the chance to go top of the league - if I remember correctly - by beating Leicester in the next midweek home game. We had beaten Liverpool, so surely Leicester would lie down like hunted-to-exhaustion vermin and accept their fate.

By this point in my Boro life I shouldn't have been surprised or disappointed, but I still was. The Foxes ran rings around the red-shirted chickens that were on the pitch that night and beat us 3-0. I left the stadium feeling completely let down, surrounded by many who just shook their heads, having long become accustomed to the bitter taste of dashed hopes. How did this happen? How was the team so completely unable to rise to the occasion? I was starting to believe what Gaz's Boro-weary, cynical father had said to me just a few games into my Boro-supporting days: "Boro will *always* let you down."

A 1-0 loss at Villa followed before the visit of another side with thorn-in-the-side potential: Southampton. It proved to be a curious affair, with a long-range goal by Pallister, a Gazza penalty and a Brian Deane goal adding up to a 3-2 win.

The early-season momentum seemed unwilling to reappear, however, and three league defeats followed to Leeds, Chelsea and Newcastle. An injection of impetus was badly needed, not to mention a good kick up the backside joined by a rocket up the arse and a flea in the lug.

It came in the form of the return of another old boy; one who still held a place in many Boro fans' hearts. I'm talking of course about Juninho. He had left at the end of that crazy 1996/97season, leaving us with the memory of him sitting alone and crying on the Elland Road turf. His spell at Atletico Madrid hadn't gone well, with the Brazilian suffering a serious injury within his first few months. Now, in October 1999, he was returning to the Boro on loan for the remainder of the season. He obviously felt some kinship with the Boro, and there was no room for doubt about the reciprocation of these feelings when a huge crowd turned up for his appearance in the reserve team at the Riverside.

His return sparked another short run of good form, with West Ham, Watford and Everton all beaten (Mr. Unfulfilled Potential / Unlucky With Injury Alun Armsrong scored his last goal for the club in the first of these). Sunderland weren't in the mood to allow this party to continue and salvaged a 1-1 draw on our turf. A shockingly bad 5-1 mauling at the hands of Arsenal followed that, and then Wimbledon came up North with little intention of playing pretty football and went home with a 0-0 draw. Bradford away finished 1-1.

Any idea of consistency either way was soon abandoned with a 2-1 home victory over Spurs followed by a 1-0 loss to Sheffield Wednesday at Hillsborough. We also found ourselves dumped out of the FA Cup by Wrexham before Christmas this season. The third round was played early this time round, I think it was because of Manchester United's extraordinary decision to drop out of the competition and play in some highly-sponsored and lucrative World Club Cup of some kind.

A lot happened over that festive season. Just before Christmas my other half seemed to develop a low-grade stomach bug that ruined her enjoyment of my company's party and even Christmas Day itself. We had no inkling of what could be causing it until one of my aunts, in the trademark blunt manner of all aunts, suggested that she could be pregnant. My auntie was right: a test confirmed this diagnosis between Christmas and New Year. I was going to be a father. I was elated and terrified in equal measure.

We spent the New Year with relatives in the Borders region of Scotland. It wasn't as remarkable for the arrival of a new millennium as for the fact that half the people at the party were suffering from a rotten flu virus. With my wife still suffering from morning sickness, it was something of a subdued affair. I did my best to keep in with the spirit of things, however, and didn't protest too much when offered yet more alcohol by my host on the first morning of the New Year. When in Rome, do as the Romans do; when in Scotland, get shit-faced.

And so the 1990s, the 20th Century and the second millennium headed for the door, with their arms linked and singing maudlin songs, presumably.

It was mid-January before the Premier League recommenced, and our reputation for good cup runs suffered even more with a fifth round defeat at the hands of Tranmere Rovers in the League Cup. Still, there was the league to play for. We had to ensure we'd still be in the Premiership next season.

The change in century and millennium didn't affect the customary New Year crapness, and an abject 4-1 home defeat to Derby County set the scene. We lost to Leicester, Manchester United and drew 0-0 with Liverpool before we were subjected to another awful home display. Aston Villa came to the Riverside on St. Valentine's Day and obviously felt in the mood to perform a footballing massacre. Boro were destroyed 4-0 and Gazza found himself sent off and injured at the same time after a reckless forearm smash to the rock-hard face of Villa's George Boateng. He broke his forearm and wouldn't play for Boro again.

Just as the fans were starting to question Bryan Robson's continued tenure as manager, the team was magically stung into action. A seven-game unbeaten run ensued, starting with a 2-0 win over Coventry. Draws with Leeds and Southampton preceded a rarest of rare gems: a home win against Arsenal. Boro played out of their skins to emerge with a 2-1 victory and prompted the inevitable, "Why can't they play like that every time?" questions.

A Ziege goal helped us gain a point at Sunderland and a young, red-haired whippet of a lad from the youth team called Andy Campbell scored the winner against Sheffield Wednesday at home. At the beginning of April we travelled down to White Hart Lane and let Ricard loose against a Spurs defence who seemed to freeze every time he played against them. That 3-2 win in the capital marked the end of the good run.

April marked another change in my own life. The daily commute to Leeds was becoming tiresome, so we had decided to sell our house in Ingelby Barwick and move to Thirsk. It was decided that this was a good, central location in the North East / Yorkshire region and was also closer to the in-laws, who would come in useful for babysitting once the baby was born.

I missed the next midweek home game against the red half of Salford because I had to attend a team-building event in Leeds with work colleagues. It was as dreadful and bullshit-festooned as it sounds, but I managed to get out of spending an entire evening with colleagues by suffering some kind of anxiety attack following my halting and nerve-wracked presentation to them. I just wasn't cut out for that stuff back then. I still don't enjoy standing up in front of people, unless I've had a few tonsil-looseners and am performing Karaoke. Anyway, my father, the United fan, took my ticket for the match and went along to watch with my wife, and had to sit on his hands through an incredible game that finished 4-3 to Manchester United. I saw the goals on TV later and was slightly gutted that I'd missed it, despite the end result.

The season was once again coming to a close. Safety from relegation was all but certain by the middle of April, but there seemed to be little chance of a top-half finish this season, despite a similar haul of points to last season's. There was an away defeat to Coventry and then a 1-1 draw at Chelsea before Brian Deane's penalty proved enough to earn maximum points against West Ham at home.

May began with yet another frustrating 2-2 draw with the black and white mob from up the road, with Juninho and Festa getting our goals. The young Robbie Stockdale earned a point at home to already-relegated Watford before Brian Deane and Juninho scored the goals that put a nice gloss to the end of the season with a 2-0 victory over the blue half of Merseyside at Goodison Park.

It was, overall, a pretty unremarkable season. A twelfth place finish (just behind Newcastle on goal difference) wasn't terrible, but there had been no improvement over the previous season, despite early optimism and decent performances. Consistency seemed to be the issue with the team; one week we were beating Arsenal, the next we were being thrashed by the likes of Derby County. The spine of a decent team were there, and it was hoped that we could hold onto this and maybe add a few more star signings to propel the club further up the Premier League.

As for the rest of the league, it was notable for a few things. Manchester United won the league by 18 points, Leeds came third and qualified for the Champions League qualifying round and Watford, Sheffield Wednesday and Wimbledon were relegated. The Dons had a new, interesting destiny ahead of them with an unprecedented geographical relocation to Milton Keynes, of all paces. The fabled days of the Crazy Gang were well and truly over.

Chapter 8 - 2000/01

In-Tel-national Rescue

Ah, the dawn of a new millennium, the 21ˢᵗ Century…just spare me the arguments about when it actually started, please…

Whatever, the 21ˢᵗ Century was here; a point in time that used to look so futuristic and distant, even in 1990. Where were the flying cars, silver boiler suits and meals in pill form that the books and films had promised us? Still in our imaginations, it seems. Of course, times were a-changing. The internet was spreading and growing, becoming more and more influential in the way we worked and played. At work we could e-mail crap jokes and preposterous urban myths to all our friends at the click of a button. At home we were able to negate the need for red-faced, surreptitious episodes in newsagents, but had to wait half an hour for anything decent to download on the dial-up connection, by which time curious wives and mothers had kicked the bedroom door down.

Still, the greater world around us moved on apace. In the news headlines we saw Pope John Paul II apologize to the world for the wrongdoings of the Roman Catholic Church over the centuries. Bless his cotton footwear. Vladimir Putin became president of Russia, presumably taking a few days to clear all the empty vodka bottles left by his predecessor from his office in the Kremlin. Israel withdrew IDF forces from Lebanon for the first time in twenty-two years, an Air France Concorde crashed into a hotel in Paris, Al Qaeda bombed the USS Cole in the Arabian Gulf and chimpanzee-in-chief George W Bush won the protracted US presidential election with some electoral jiggery-pokery to do with hanging chads in Florida

The biggest films of the year included Tom Cruise in *Mission Impossible II*, Ridley Scott's *Gladiator* and a bearded Tom Hanks in *Cast Away*. The world of popular music featured a generational battle of the divas between Britney and Madonna, and U2's *Beautiful Day* marked a return to form for Bono and the boys. Music snobs go back to your Peruvian goat nostril blowing, please.

In other sport and football, France won Euro 2000 with a golden goal, Real Madrid won their eighth European Cup/Champions League title, Tiger Woods achieved the golfing Grand Slam, that German fella won the F1 Championship, Pete Sampras bored his way to another Wimbledon tennis victory and Italy joined the Five Nations Rugby union tournament to make it the Six Nations and finally gave Scotland someone to beat. I conveniently forget that I'm half Scottish sometimes. Sassenach bastard.

For me, 2000 was a year of massive change. There was the move to Thirsk, my thirtieth birthday and – the biggest one of all – the arrival of my son in the middle of August. Everything changed at that point: I was now responsible for a new life, one that I would nurture and mould. It scared me half to death, and ten years later I still can't quite believe it happened.

I had to give up my season ticket, of course. Of course?! Well, there were many factors here, which I won't go into in case it sounds like I'm making excuses. I was able to keep my Sky Sports subscription, at least, and would be able to keep up with Boro's fortunes via the various mediums available. The gentle tones of Alistair Brownlee and Century Radio were stored as preset number one on the car radio.

As for the football itself, the fans of Middlesbrough FC had reason to be optimistic about the new season. We lost Christian Ziege to Liverpool under controversial circumstances, but this was off-set by the arrival of Alen Boksic, Christian Karembeu, Ugo Ehiogu (albeit in November) and Joseph Desire-Job. Boksic was another example of Bryan Robson's ability to attract top-drawer talent to the club. Would his coaching skills measure up as well? After something of a sterile, uneventful season, Boro fans were looking for some excitement. I'm not sure what transpired was what they had in mind.

It all started so promisingly as well. The first game of the season, less than a week after my son's birth, was away to Coventry. We stuffed them 3-1 with Job and Boksic sharing the goals. Here comes that hope again. You can't do anything about it; it gets into your head, even though you know where it is going to end up.

A draw with Spurs was followed by a 2-1 home defeat to Dirty Leeds, and the hope was soon receding. An indifferent run of form was becoming established: draws with the odd defeat as Derby, Villa and Manchester City shared points with us and Everton doomed us to yet another narrow home defeat. Southampton away provided a measure of respite with a 3-1 win and a brace of Boksic goals. It was becoming painfully obvious that Mr. Boksic had class and skill oozing from every pore, but he seemed to keep it hidden a lot of the time because he just couldn't be arsed, apparently. He would also develop a reputation for being injury prone, and the cynical whisperings about his reportedly astronomical weekly wage of 63,000 quid were soon heard in the pubs and work places of Teesside.

A wretched run of eight league defeats and one draw then followed, starting with a 3-1 beating by the Geordies. Goals were hard to come by at the right end, but flew in with joyful abandon at the other. Charlton, Ipswich, Arsenal, Manchester United, Leicester all took great pleasure in adding to this horrible run. The fans' patience was running out fast. A team with such talent just shouldn't have been struggling so badly and losing so poorly to average teams. There was also another early exit in the League cup, with an aggregate defeat to lowly Macclesfield.

At the end of November, fellow strugglers Bradford City were the visitors to the Riverside and promptly went into a 2-0 lead. Booing started to echo round the stadium; a sound I hadn't heard a lot of in my Boro life to date. Mr. Robson's future at the club was starting to look decidedly uncertain. Ehiogu and Ince scored in the second half to salvage a point, but it didn't stop Boro sinking to nineteenth place in the Premier League. The crowds at the Riverside were noticeably lower, threatening to dip below 28,000. Something had to change.

An away defeat to West Ham marked Bryan Robson's last game as sole manager of the team. Chairman Steve Gibson decided against the nuclear option of sacking him and, after some hard negotiations, brought in the much-needed acumen and smooth demeanour of former England manager Terry Venables. There were opinions galore as to what his actual role was, but it was clear that he had been asked to come in to take the reins and offer some guidance and advice to Robson. Where that left Robson was uncertain; would he be able to resume sole management duties at some point? He was, as they say, damaged goods in many people's eyes.

Venables' first game at the (joint) helm was another defeat, away to Sunderland on 9th December. Boro were now rock bottom in 20th place in the league. The only way was up from there. The influence of any new manager usually takes a little bit of time to show, but Venables concentrated on a back-to-basics approach, tightening up the permeable defence. The team conceded only two goals in the next seven league games, having let in twelve in the previous seven. Starting the revival with a home win (the first of the season) against Chelsea, they even managed to avoid the traditional post-Christmas blues and went on a ten-game unbeaten run, gradually dragging themselves up and away from the bottom of the table and towards safety.

The FA Cup didn't prove to be much of a distraction from the primary mission of survival. Hamilton Ricard scored with a superb curling effort to help us progress against Bradford in round three, but in the next round Wimbledon knocked us out in a replay at Selhurst Park.

In the league even big teams such as Liverpool found the newly-tightened defence a difficult proposition and were sent away without points. Goals were still at a premium at the other end, however - aside from a 4-0 win over Derby – and seven of the ten games in the unbeaten run were draws, but that was much better than suffering defeat after mind-numbing defeat, and the points total was looking much, much healthier. The last game of the run was against Villa away, where Ehiogu scored against his former club to secure a 1-1 draw.

The next league defeat suffered was at home to Southampton on 24th February, but by then Boro were out of the bottom three. March started with a 0-0 draw against Charlton Athletic, and then it was time for the annual visit to St. James' Park in Newcastle. Newcastle were now a comfortable mid-table outfit, still hoping they could become a permanent fixture amongst the big boys at the top end, but ultimately falling short. Even Bobby Robson's management couldn't help them break out of their indolence and Boro were not in a charitable mood on this particular visit. Alen Boksic decided to turn up on this particular occasion, scoring with a magical free-kick to give us a rare taste of victory on Geordie turf.

Chelsea beat us 2-1 at Stamford Bridge in the next game, and this was followed by a 0-0 draw with that other North East team from Wearside. We then expected nothing less than our customary battering at Highbury by Wenger's Arsenal, but contrived to win the game 3-0 despite having only one or two shots on target in the whole match. It was an extraordinary example of bare-faced smash-and-grab, with two of the goals being own goals. All that mattered at the end of the match was that an unlikely victory was secured and top-flight safety was within reach.

A first goal by late-season arrival Dean Windass wasn't enough to prevent a home defeat to Ipswich, but at least we were back on familiar territory: beating a team like Arsenal and then losing to Ipswich. This is a little unfair to the Tractor Boys, to be honest. They had come up from the First Division for this season and were expected to bounce straight back down, but eventually finished fifth and qualified for the UEFA Cup.

Leicester away provided one of the most memorable Boro goals in recent years, with the enigmatic Mr. Boksic turning a defender this way and that before delivering an exquisite lob into the goal from more than twenty yards out. Ince and Ricard added the other goals in a 3-0 win that took us up to fifteenth in the table. A 2-0 home defeat to Manchester United – on their way to a seventh Premiership title – was follow by a 1-1 draw with already-relegated Bradford City.

Safety had been secured well before West Ham came to visit the North East for the last game of the season. Job and Karembeu scored in the 2-1 victory, but what happened after the game is more memorable. As the team and the management staff performed their traditional end-of-season lap of honour, there was clearly-audible hostility and discontent directed towards Bryan Robson from the stands. It was clear that he wasn't going to be able to continue working at the club in any capacity. He had brought some exciting times and big players to the club, of that there was little doubt, but ultimately his coaching skills had been found to be lacking. It was time for both Robson and the club to move on.

In the end Boro had finished a comfortable fourteenth after that uncomfortable flirtation with relegation. Uncertainty now stood like the awkward shy man in the corner at a party, waiting for someone to tell him where to find a drink. Who would be the manager next season? Would Venables stay on as sole manager? Would the real Alen Boksic please step forward? At least we weren't in the shoes of Manchester City, who joined the Cities of Coventry and Bradford in relegation. There was something to build on.

As for me, I had challenges of my own. I fought through massive sleep deprivation and the appearance of an irregular heart-beat (too many caffeine products, I think) and tried my utmost to be a good father and husband. My son was still just a noisy pooping and eating machine, but I was looking forward to being able to impose my world view on the boy when he became old enough to pay attention to my foibles. For now a Boro romper suit and a cuddly Roary the Lion would have to do.

Chapter 9

2001/02 – A SMAC Odyssey

What can be said about 2001? Everyone I know remembers where they were when the shocking events of that bright September morning in New York unfolded. The whole world watched as the whole world changed. I was at work in an office in the old York when the news came through and almost everyone in the office spent the rest of the day vainly searching the internet for news about the attacks and listening to increasingly wild and wacky rumours and theories before going home to watch the aftermath on the rolling news coverage.

These history-defining moments overshadow everything else, especially frivolous games involving chasing a stitched leather bag of air around a field. Perspective is brought quickly and painfully into focus. Eventually, the shock and horror fade and recede in our minds, and the paralysis of fear gives way to stoic acceptance that life has to go on…trite as that sounds. We soon go back to worrying about our own worlds and lives; wondering what is for tea tonight and wondering how that ball-kicking game at the weekend will go…

The other news events of the year seem irrelevant in comparison to 9/11, but the notable events included the UK Foot and Mouth outbreak, the re-election of Blair's Labour party into power, the execution of Timothy McVeigh (two months before 9/11) and the bankruptcy of Enron.

In popular culture, the world of film was dominated by fantasy and animation. The first *Harry Potter* and *The Lord of The Rings* films led the way, with *Monsters, Inc.* and *Shrek* in tow. In the music world, US-based "Nu Metal" and the likes of Linkin Park and Limp Bizkit featured heavily, and the Beatles "1" album showed that the appetite for Liverpudlian boy bands wasn't diminishing. Oh, and Steps split up. What a Tragedy.

The inevitable departure of Bryan Robson was not seen as a tragedy. He had overseen six seasons of mixed success and rollercoaster emotions. Early promise had been unfulfilled. He had come so close to, yet so far from, making history with the club. The consensus was that he had been found wanting in terms of his coaching ability.

It's possible that Gibson agreed with this assessment. When it became clear that Terry Venables wasn't going to stick around, the chairman went looking for a new man to take the helm. Steve McClaren, who had earned a reputation as a good coach and assistant manager with Derby County and Manchester United, was approached and turned down offers to join Southampton and West Ham to take up the challenge of managing Boro.

McClaren's first bit of business in the transfer market was to buy Gareth Soughate from Aston Villa. The signing was seen as something of a coup given his undoubted quality as a central defender. It was an exciting prospect for Boro fans to contemplate the reunited Southgate/Ehiuogu partnership at the heart of the defence, and a couple of Manchester United second-string players in the form of Jonathan Greening and Mark Wilson were also added. Szilard Nemeth, the Slovakian forward, joined from Inter Bratislava, and the French full-back Franck Queudrue also signed. The Boro public weren't sure what to expect, but were hopeful that someone of McClaren's obvious coaching calibre would bring success. The more instant the success was the better, naturally.

It didn't start very well, unfortunately. McClaren's first game in charge at the Riverside saw the visit of Arsenal, who went about their usual business of giving us a pasting at the Riverside and promptly condemned Boro to a humiliating 4-0 defeat. There followed two away games at Bolton and Everton, both of which were lost, before we entertained the black and white beer bellies from up the road.

We started that game quite well, as it happens, but a couple of key refereeing decisions concerning penalties at either end and a sending off turned the tide in Newcastle's favour. They romped to a 4-1 win in the end, leaving Boro fans worried about how this season was going to pan out. So much for a good coach. Goals were flying in to the Boro net with alarming ease, and only one had been scored at the right end…by a defender.

The recovery started with a 2-0 win over West Ham at home (the weekend after the horrifying events in the USA), followed by a hard-fought comeback in the televised Monday night match against Leicester City. We came from a goal down at half-time to win 2-1, with goals from Ince and new boy Greening.

Next up was Chelsea away – always a tricky prospect – but Boksic and Robbie Stockdale scored the goals that earned a creditable 2-2 draw. The early-season crapness was fast becoming a distant memory...or so we thought. That perennial not-so-much-bogey-as-constant-stream-of-snot team called Southampton mugged us 3-1 at home. The revival was well and truly over, before it had really got going.

After the international break in early October, Boro resumed with a 0-0 draw away to Charlton Athletic and an always-pleasant home win against Sunderland on a Monday night, with French Franck showing us his mercurial ability with free kicks. We then lost 2-1 away to Tottenham, settling into a familiar, arrhythmic pattern of inconsistency. The prevalent feeling was that the team just couldn't get into top gear. Maybe they were struggling with the new manager's almost scientific approach, but they seemed unable to play free-flowing football for any more than the odd patch.

Something clicked on 3rd November, however, and Boro gave Derby their customary hammering at our place; 5-1 on this occasion. Nemeth, Boksic and Mustoe got a goal each, but the star of the show was the young man called Carlos Marinelli, who scored twice and ran the Rams ragged. As seems to happen with many players hailing from Argentina, this young fellow was immediately saddled with the expectation that he would be the next Maradona. Other than in this Derby game, I don't recall him ever looking like he would get close to fulfilling such a destiny.

The team obviously exhausted all their good form in that game, because other than a 1-0 win away at Blackburn, there were no further victories to celebrate in 2001. Since the last four games in December were against Manchester United, Liverpool, Arsenal and a resurgent Newcastle, one can't be too surprised about this. Disappointed, yes; surprised, no. A fourth round exit from the League Cup at the hands of Blackburn Rovers did little to lift the mood.

Christmas 2001 was a big family affair for me and my little brood. We travelled up to the wilds of the Perthshire countryside in Scotland to spend Christmas Day at my aunt and uncle's guest house with various members of my extended family. We had a light sprinkling of snow to get us in the mood, and my one-year-old son didn't seem too bothered about being kitted out in the full Boro kit that Father

Christmas brought him. My father, on the other hand, didn't look too impressed. At the end of the day, I was brain-washer-in-chief, and I was just doing my job, while I could still influence the poor boy.

2002 started with a New Year's Day fixture at home against Everton. Boro folk hero Gianluca Festa scored the only goal in a 1-0 win, and then it was time for the FA Cup third round. Boro weren't to get an easy ride in this competition, drawing Wimbledon away, but managed a 0-0 draw to set up a replay at home. In said replay, old Leeds boy Noel Whelan started his best run of form for the club, adding to a Cunningham own goal to earn a 2-0 win and a fourth round tie with McClaren's former employers, Manchester United.

Consistently inconsistent as ever, Boro lost 2-1 at the Al-Fayed-funded Premiership new boys Fulham in the next league game, before drawing 1-1 at home to Bolton. Whelan was on the score-sheet once again.

The following weekend saw the visit of Manchester United in the FA cup. The game was shown live on TV, and everyone expected a full house, but the fans apparently took a stand against the pricing for the game, and only 17,000 turned up to watch. Many regretted their decision later, because Boro managed to pull of something of an upset, repelling the Manchester United attack and scoring two late goals. Noel Whelan's goal – latching onto a mistake by United's veteran French centre-back, Laurent Blanc – was followed by a Leeds salute towards the joyous (if half-empty) North Stand. His feelings towards the red half of Manchester were plain to see.

Whelan scored again to give us a 1-0 victory at the Stadium of Light on the following Tuesday night. We had yet another 0-0 draw with Charlton, then a 2-2 draw at home with mega-bucks trophy-chasers (remember those days?) Leeds United, Ince and the veteran loan star Dean Windass grabbing the goals. A 2-1 win at home to Fulham in midweek was followed by a 1-0 defeat at the Boleyn ground in 'appy 'ammer territory, resuming that staccato pattern of draws, wins and losses.

At least the form in the FA Cup was holding up. Blackburn Rovers were the next team to be beaten, 1-0 at the Riverside in mid-February. The keenly-watched quarter final draw threw up the rather chewy prospect of Everton. There had been no easy draws at all.

Leicester visited the Riverside in early March and very kindly scored the winning goal for Boro. The hapless Frank Sinclair slotted the ball past his own 'keeper from a good 30 yards to the amazement and delight of the Boro fans. Southampton away (on a Wednesday night – credit to the fans who travelled for that one) were next up, and Noel Whelan scored again to secure a 1-1 draw for us.

The following weekend was the FA Cup quarter final against Everton, which was won much more easily than expected. Whelan, Nemeth and Ince scored in a comfortable but unspectacular 3-0 win. The match was televised once again, but this time there was a larger crowd of over 26,000. Attendances for the season had settled at between 26 and 30 thousand depending on the opposition. Was that something to do with the football on show? McClaren's style definitely wasn't flashy, all-out attack and he did have a strange tendency to say the word "magnificent" in every single post-match interview, but the goals against column was showing a satisfactory number.

The lower attendances could probably be put down to a combination of factors, such as the quality of football being played and the increasing prices to watch a game. Of course there will always be people who trot out the old, "if you want entertainment, go to the bloody circus," line. I'm sure some would wag would reply that the defence had at times acted like clowns this season. As for me, well I didn't get to go to many matches this season. Family commitments made it difficult to justify the cost of a season ticket, but I was at least thankful that many of the games were shown on TV.

Liverpool visited the Riverside next and were once again sent back to Merseyside without a point. The Riverside has proved to be a lean hunting ground for the Scouse team. Gareth Southgate scored the winning goal in the 2-1 triumph: his first for the club. Then it was time to visit Old Trafford, which no longer seemed an unbreakable fortress after the spectacular win there in 1999. Our emergence as something of a bogey team to United on their own turf was enhanced with a 1-0 win in front of the largest crowd of the season in the Premiership. The recently-arrived-on-loan Benito Carbone made the most of a defensive mistake and set up Alen Boksic to slide home the winner. I don't think Roy Keane was very happy with his team mates that day. I'm sure there were some bulging veins on temples that night.

March finished with a 1-1 draw at home to Spurs, courtesy of another goal by the French full-back. Robbie Mustoe gave us a 1-0 victory against Derby County on 1st April, and then Carbone and Ehiogu scored to defeat Aston Villa at the Riverside. Boro were up to ninth position in the table.

Next up it was Arsenal in the FA Cup semi-final. The Gooners were on course for another double-winning season under the selectively-myopic Arsene Wenger. Boro's team was ravaged by injury and had to call on youngsters like Luke Wilkshire, the Australian winger, to fill in. The Boro contingent went to Old Trafford full of hope more than expectation, but organized a card display to demonstrate their kinship and feelings of communal pride. I wasn't there myself, but watched it on TV. The card display and the singing were incredibly inspiring, making those of us watching at home feel proud, and it must have rubbed off on the team.

Boro battled their hearts out against the London aristocrats, not letting them settle or play their normal game. There were one or two half-chances created, but ultimately spurned. Hope was kept alive and kicking until an Arsenal corner was diverted into the Boro goal by Gianluca Festa. Thierry Henry, who had taken the corner, strutted around like Freddy bloody Mercury in celebration of the own goal, right in front of the Boro fans. The distraught Festa sank to his knees. All we needed was a robe, a crown and a guillotine.

And that was that. There was no coming back. Arsenal went on to get their league and cup double and Boro's season petered out. Home defeats to Blackburn and Chelsea were joined by away defeats to Leeds and soon-to-be-relegated Ipswich Town.

So Middlesbrough finished twelfth on forty-five points. It wasn't bad; it wasn't great. It was OK. Given the way the season had started, things could have been worse. The unexpected FA Cup run had given fans something to cheer, but it was obvious that there was still work to do. Steve McClaren was still trying to stamp his mark on the team and obviously had a few ageing and ridiculously-paid Robson-era stars like Mr. Boksic to deal with. He wasn't exactly winning all the fans over, either. He was still working with the England team and involved in their preparations for the World Cup in Japan and South Korea, and there were rumours in the press about him considering an offer to manage Leeds United. He was obviously an ambitious man, and had some work to do to convince Boro fans of his loyalty and commitment.

Then it was summer again. I took my wife and son on holiday to the scorching hot island of Corfu and while I watched the World Cup games in a bar by the brilliant Mediterranean Sea, I didn't know what was looming round the corner for me and my family. Not far from where England were being dumped out of the competition by Brazil, something like the beat of a butterfly's wings and a slight shift in tectonic plates started a chain of events that would once more take me on my travels.

I do love a bit of Chaos Theory…

Chapter 10 - 2002/03

Faraway, so close...

2002 began with the issue of Euro notes and coins in countries that had signed up to the single currency, and retailers and restaurant owners around the continent rejoiced as they surreptitiously banged all their prices up. Slobodan Milosevic went on trial for war crimes at The Hague and the dear and very old Queen Mum died at the very ripe age of 101. The US State Department named the seven countries it deemed to be in the Axis of Evil, terrorists attacked a nightclub in Bali killing over two hundred people, and the UN Security Council unanimously passed resolution 1441.

In the world of entertainment, Eminem, Shakira and Britney Spears jockeyed for top album sales, and sequels in the *Lord of the Rings*, *Harry Potter* and *Star Wars* franchises were big at the box office.

In other sport and the non-Boro sphere of football, we saw Brazil lift another World Cup in Japan and South Korea and Real Madrid won their sixth European Cup (or whatever it was called in 2002). Lleyton Hewitt and Serena Williams triumphed in the tennis at the All England Club and Schumacher won the Formula 1 championship for the third year running. A lot of sequels and repeats this year, then.

For me and my family, 2002 was a big year. I was once more destined to leave these shores for life-enrichment and a tax-free salary. But more on that later.

Boro started the season full of expectation once more. The big-money, record-breaking signing of Massimo Maccarone from Empoli showed real ambition and intent. The young Italian had impressed in a recent U21 international tournament, including a game against England. The Cameroonian right-back/midfielder, Geremi, joined on a season-long loan spell from Real Madrid, combative Dutch midfielder George Boateng was signed from Villa, and last but not least, a certain diminutive Brazilian joined Middlesbrough for his third, and hopefully luckiest, spell.

And so the season started. Everyone was desperate to get off to a better start than last time round, and a 0-0 draw away to the Saints of Southampton was secured on opening day, 17th August. A week later we had our first home game of the season against Fulham and Maccarone scored twice to put Boro into a good position, only for two very late goals to spoil the mood. Amends were made in the next home game, with Joseph "One" Job "On Teesside" grabbing the only goal of the game against Blackburn Rovers. Perspective again threw the custard pie of reality into our faces as Manchester United beat us 1-0 at Old Trafford.

As the summer of 2002 faded and autumn's chill moved in, I found myself approached by a firm of consultants in London who were looking for people to work in the Far East. The wanderlust instilled in me from childhood was still as keen and as curious as ever, and my initial interest was soon taking more tangible form, taking me down to London for meetings with company directors and talking on the phone to people in faraway Taiwan. I don't know how it happened so quickly, really, but before I knew it I was being offered a well-paid job in Taiwan working on the high-profile High Speed Rail project, and both the money and the opportunity for career advancement were tempting. The only problem was that I would be going alone, leaving my wife and young son at home. I was sure that I would be able to get home every few months, or get the family out to Taiwan for visits, and knew that both my wife's parents and my own parents were on close at hand to offer support. I hoped that the internet would also provide a good way to stay in touch.

Football is a mere distraction when such things are going on in one's life, but they can be a good distraction. The Mackems visited the Riverside on a Tuesday night in early September and were put to the sword with a 3-0 defeat. Nemeth and the exciting-looking Maccarone scored the goals. Any notion of gaining early-season momentum was soon pooh-poohed with an away defeat at Everton. Birmingham City were next up at home and French Franck got the only goal of the game to give us a 1-0 home win.

The next away game was a visit to the North London home of Tottenham Hotspurs. The team really gelled that day and came away with a 3-0 win, including goals by Maccarone, Geremi and Joseph Job. The messageboards were buzzing with breathless accounts of a stunning display that blew the opponents away, with comparisons to the likes of Real Madrid. Boro fans are never shy of getting carried away; positively or negatively depending on a given result. In the

League Cup, we saw a young side beat Brentford 4-1 on their turf, featuring a goal from an exciting new talent coming through the ranks in the shape of Stewart Downing.

Into October we went, and the three league games produced a win at home to Bolton, a 1-0 reverse away to Charlton Athletic and a hard-fought 2-2 draw against Leeds. The league cup run was to fall away with a whimper as we were dumped out by Ipswich Town at Portman Road. But in October I wasn't really paying much attention to what Boro were doing, other than a perfunctory glance at the internet or newspapers to see what the results were. By the end of the month I had left the UK's shores once more and had flown 8,000 miles east to the small island of Taiwan, just off the coast of China. Not for the first time in my life I landed in a strange country and wondered what the hell I was doing. My wife and child, my parents and brother and all my friends were so, so far away from me, and I was so far away from them. I hoped it would be worth it.

I managed to make some new friends quite quickly, as you have to in these situations. I was introduced to the work hard/play hard (OK, maybe look like you're working hard) style of life in that part of the world, and was pleased to find that Premiership football was quite easily accessible on TV in the Far East, even if it meant staying in various bars until silly o'clock to watch the matches kicking off at 3pm in the UK. In the four or so years since I'd been in the USA, worldwide coverage of English football had improved considerably, and there was an obvious appetite for the game in that part of the world, going by the number of replica shirts being worn by the Taiwanese I saw in the bars watching games.

It must be said that every shirt I saw was from one of the so-called Big Four teams like Manchester United, Liverpool, Arsenal and soon-to-be-Russian-billionaire-funded Chelsea. Watching games against the Big Four was particularly hard, especially if they scored and dozens of Taiwanese chaps jumped up for joy. I doubted that any of them had actually been to a match, and felt justified in judging them as nothing more than the worst kind glory supporters, especially now that I'd had a good seven or eight years supporting a *proper* team under my belt, with all the emotional investment that this came with.

I've been to lots of games and had seen my team relegated, for God's sake. Now sit down and pipe down before I say something cutting in a heavy Boro accent. Even if you don't understand a word of it, like.

I was glad that the advances in technology not only allowed me to keep in touch with family and friends, but also kept me in the loop with the vibrant Boro messageboard scene on the likes of Fly Me To The Moon's website. In the quiet periods between editing letters for Japanese engineers, I found myself having early-morning debates about football, music, religion and politics with night-shifters and other Boro exiles. It kept me relatively sane.

For Boro, November was a real topsy-turvy ride, with two wins and three losses. Newcastle, Chelsea and West Brom beat us at their grounds, whilst Liverpool and Man City were beaten at home. Southgate, Geremi, Ehiogu and Boksic chipped in with some goals, but the early promise of the young Italian stallion known as Maccarone was becoming a distant memory. He was apparently struggling with the physical aspects of the English game and hadn't scored since the end of September.

Into December we dashed, in a bright, blinged-up yellow sleigh driven by a Betel-nut chewing crazy taxi driver, and life as a bar-propping, internet-addicted expat was becoming almost bearable. I was doing my best to keep myself busy and keep the lonely times to a minimum. Boro came up against a triumvirate of London teams in the first half of the month, drawing 2-2 with the 'ammers, 1-1 at home with Chelsea and losing 2-0 away to the Arsenal. The Chelsea home game was one that I watched on a TV in a bar called Saints and Sinners. I sat myself as far away from the Taipei branch of the Chelsea Supporters club as I could and gave a good, long lusty cheer when Geremi twatted home a glorious free kick for us.

As Christmas approached I found myself mixing with diplomats at ultra-posh black-tie events, meaning I had to hunt around Hong Kong for a black dinner suit during a visa-run weekend there. It was all a bit of a blur; my main focus was on getting home to see my family again, and the weekend before Christmas itself I boarded a Cathay Pacific flight home via Hong Kong, enduring one of the scariest and bumpiest flights of my life on the first hour-long leg, before spending nearly fourteen hours in the air all the way back to London Heathrow. By the time I got home to Thirsk I was shattered but ridiculously happy to be there. I had actually gone home a day or two earlier than I'd said I would be going. I'm a sucker for little surprises like that.

Christmas was everything it should be: happy and superb, despite my wife and I falling foul of a stomach bug that made us a bit sick for a few days. I was actually supposed to head back to Taiwan before the New Year, but because of the bug I was able to stay home for a few days more and see the turn of the year with my loved ones and some friends who came round for the night. I also got to watch the televised Boxing Day match against Manchester United, and a memorable one it was too. Boksic, on one of his good days, gave us the lead in the first half before Nemeth showed an amazing burst of pace and strength to charge into the area and blast the ball home. Any threat of a comeback was quashed with a late Job goal, and it finished 3-1. McClaren had got one over on his old boss, Ferguson.

On 2nd January 2003 I headed back east. We were planning a visit to Taiwan by my wife in around March or April. We weren't aware then of the other little surprise I had left, or indeed of the way things would transpire later that year.

Boro started the New Year in the way they start every post-Christmas campaign: poorly. It's as traditional as the sprouts and tinsel on Teesside. The last game of 2002 was lost 1-0 at Villa, before the same result did for us at Blackburn on New Year's Day. Chelsea dumped us out of the FA Cup at the first hurdle (again 1-0) before we managed to get a 2-2 draw with Southampton at home. Maccarone finally remembered what we'd paid over 8 million quid for and gave us a goal to cheer. Fulham beat us 1-0 at Craven Cottage (we were consistent at least), before Aston Villa paid us a visit just a month after our visit to Villa Park and subjected Boro to a 5-2 humiliation. Nice.

There were only two league games in February: a 1-1 draw with the red half of Liverpool at Anfield, thanks to another Geremi goal, and a first win of the year at the Stadium of Light, 3-1 against Sunderland. New central defender Chris Riggott contributed a brace of goals, and Malcolm Christie, another ex-Derby County recruit got the other. It's always a sweet feeling to do the Mackems over in their own back yard.

What wasn't sweet was what happened in my own life in February 2003. It started on a high, but ended on the lowest of the lows. That little surprise I had unwittingly left revealed itself in the form of an overjoyed and pregnant wife ringing me with the good news, but only a few weeks later she rang me while I was out with my colleagues and friends to tell me that she had miscarried.

I felt every possible emotion that night, but guilt was by far the biggest one. I should have been there for her and wasn't. I couldn't face the loneliness of my apartment that night, so stayed with my friends for another hour or two. They insisted on taking me to one of our favourite bars: a small, intimate venue with a good music collection where we could stay as long as we liked. I sat there, not really wanting to drink anything, I was just glad of the company. The DJ put on Coldplay's *The Scientist* and the lyrics of that song made me cry like a child that night.

I spent the next few days agonising over whether to just go home there and then. In hindsight I wish I had been stronger and done so. I was eight years younger and more foolish back then, but after several long talks to my wife and my mother I felt assured that she was being supported at home and that it wouldn't be too difficult to wait a few more weeks until late March when she was due to come out for her visit. The one decision I did make quite promptly was that I wouldn't stay in Taiwan for the long term. Such things have a way of bringing what is truly important in life into sharp and unforgiving focus. I told my boss on his next visit from Singapore the following week, and he fully understood, but asked that I stay on until they found a replacement for me. I agreed to do so, but would later come to regret it.

The rest of the football season passed me by, to be fair. There was a win against the Geordies in the match rearranged following a controversial bad weather postponement back in December, and a superb 3-2 win at Elland Road, but I can't really remember much else, to be honest. We finished eleventh, which wasn't bad and we never really looked in danger of being sucked into a relegation battle. Manchester United won their eighth English Premier League title. Big deal.

But then this chapter isn't really about football anymore. Other, more important things were on my mind, and I ended up waiting until June that year to get back home. My wife spent a very nice week with me in Taiwan and I made sure she was made an enormous fuss of as we spent much of the week in high-end hotels and travelled around seeing the country. The setback we had been through brought us closer together than ever and my determination to get home as soon as possible grew and grew. My replacement was supposed to arrive in April, and I had naively undertaken to give a month's handover to the new arrival. It didn't really merit a month in the first place, and to make matters worse, I ended up being stuck in the country during the SARS outbreak, meaning my replacement wasn't able to travel until the outbreak was sufficiently under control.

In the meantime, most of the locals went about their business as usual, but wore surgical masks in a futile attempt to ward off airborne germs. I even saw one chap on the street take his mask down to take a long drag on a cigarette. At work we had to have our temperatures taken as we entered the office. I'm not sure what would have happened if we had a fever; maybe we would have been carted off to hospital post haste. Other than one or two who had scares with coughs and sneezes, I didn't actually encounter anyone who got SARS.

During those last two months I was in a very, very dark place. I wanted to get home desperately but wasn't able to, and everything seemed to be conspiring to keep my in Taiwan. In my final week in that extraordinary country there were two minor but noticeable earthquakes, and my mental state was as shaky as the ground I was standing on. The relief I felt when I finally boarded the plane for Hong Kong was beyond anything I've felt for quite a while.

And there we have it. 2002/2003 was something of a pivotal and "interesting" year in my own life to say the least, but nothing really spectacular when it comes to Middlesbrough Football Club. A steady second season for the new boss. Were there tectonic shifts to come in the following season? You bet.

Chapter 11 - 2003/04

We DID overcome.

2003, eh? War, eh? What is it good for, eh, huh? Securing hydrocarbons and keeping the military industrial complex in business, that's what. Other headlines this year: Shuttle Columbia tragically disintegrated on re-entry in February, Hu (not who) became the president of China, Concorde retired from active service, the Libyan Al Megrahi was jailed for the Lockerbie bombing and Bob Hope died at the ripe old age of 100.

Film highlights of the year included the likes of *The Lord of The Rings: Return of The King, Finding Nemo, The Matrix Reloaded: Franchises Are Marvelous* and *Pirates of The Caribbean: The Curse of the Black Pearl*. The music world was dominated by "Fiddy" Fifty Cent, Linkin Park, Beyonce and Coldplay.

The highlight of non-football sport had to be the England Rugby Union team's triumph in the World Cup. Jonny Wilkinson's extra-time drop-goal in Sydney against the Aussies was a sweet, sweet moment. Some German won the driving procession championship again, and a Swiss chap called Roger won the tennis at Wimbledon. Lovely.

As I've already mentioned, 2003 didn't start well personally, and I was stuck in Taiwan until the summer. When I finally got home I spent a brilliant summer with my wife and son, making up for all that lost time. I flitted around from one contract job to another, but was just glad to be back where I belonged.

Of course, the other little bonus of being home was being able to watch football "in the flesh" or even just at an earthly hour. I also had a son who was now approaching an age where he could kick a ball and was happy to sit and watch a match on the TV without running away whenever I jumped up or shouted at the screen. Best of all, he was still pliable and open to brainwashing...I mean influence. I made absolutely sure he was being steered towards a strong and unbreakable love of the Boro.

Boro went in to the new season with the addition of Bolo Zenden on loan from Chelsea and Gaizka Mendieta on loan from Lazio (via Barcelona in some weird, convoluted arrangement), and were looking to consolidate on the mid-table mediocrity of the previous term. The season didn't start too well, however, and we had to endure defeats to Fulham away, another spanking by Arsene's bunch at the Riverside and a home defeat to Leeds, not to mention a 2-0 defeat at Bolton and the 0-0 draw at Leicester. There was no league victory until 21st September at home to Everton, which ended 1-0 thanks to Mr. Job. A home win in the Carling League Cup against Brighton started off a little cup run in front of a rather meagre home crowd of just over 10,000 people.

Average crowds had continued to drop in the league as well, with the average now at around 30,000. Maybe some fans weren't overly enamoured with what they perceived as McClaren's rather functional and unexciting brand of football. Maybe the prices were starting to get too steep for the average inhabitant of Teesside. There were also a few people who complained that they thought the stewarding in the ground had become a touch too zealous. The high-viz jacket brigade were apparently too eager to clamp down on people doing things like standing up, blinking or breathing in an aggressive manner.

A 1-0 away win at Southampton ended September on a high note, but October proved to be quite a barren month for league points, courtesy of home defeats by Chelsea and Newcastle and a 0-0 draw away at Spurs. I watched the Chelsea match on a TV in an Irish bar in Barcelona, having been persuaded by Gaz and his merry band to spend good money on attending a stag weekend in a foreign city, where the cultural highlight was spending silly amounts of Euros in a bar on Las Ramblas.

To be fair, it was an enjoyable weekend, and a large splinter group decided to go and watch Barcelona play Valencia (pronounced *Barthelona verthuth Valenthia* for added authenticity) at the Stadio Camp Nou, which could be classed as a cultural experience at a stretch. The match was an impressive spectacle from our vantage point at almost the highest seating area in the stadium behind the goal. Ronaldinho was playing for the Catalonians, but we could barely make him out from up there in the Gods. There were clouds in the way, I'm sure of it, and God kept going to get more beer. As it was, Barca were shite and lost 1-0. Crazy boys.

League cup progress continued with a win away at Wigan Athletic, thanks to a rare goal from Maccarone and the winner from Mendieta in a 2-1 win. Mendieta was again on the scoresheet in a 2-0 home win against Wolverhampton Wanderers. A satisfying away win at Aston Villa was achieved with goals from Bolo Zenden and new recruit Michael Ricketts, who joined from Bolton Wanderers. Boro were up to twelfth in the league by now, and the early-season dodginess was pretty much forgotten about. A 0-0 draw at home to Liverpool was followed by an almost apologetically brazen piece of smash-and-grab football and a 1-0 win at Manchester City thanks to an own goal by Sun Jihai. The own goal was the only effort (intended or otherwise) on the City goal in the entire game.

It was around this time, in early November, that my wife and I felt safe telling our friends and family the happy news that she was pregnant once again. We had held off for the first three months, keeping fingers crossed and lips sealed until we felt that the riskiest time had passed. The baby was due to be born in the early summer of 2004. Oh good, thought I, another Boro fan to be moulded.

In the fourth round of the Carling Cup, Boro faced Everton at home. No goals were scored in normal or extra time, so it was down to the Russian roulette of the penalty shoot-out. It was the first such denouement I had witnessed as a Boro fan and I listened to it on Century Radio, biting my nails down to the quick. Aussie legend Mark Schwarzer came through magnificently, making a couple of great saves to give us a route into the quarter finals. We were suddenly dreaming of a place in the final.

December continued with two home games in the league against Portmsouth and Charlton, games we had every right to believe were winnable, and which could lift us well into the top half of the Premier League. Of course, typical Boro weren't going to let any such belief or sense of entitlement influence them and both games were drawn 0-0. Boro briefly reached ninth position after the game with Pompey, but fell back to eleventh after the Charlton match.

Tottenham laid in wait in the quarter finals of the league cup, and we found ourselves having to rely on penalties again after a 1-1 draw. It was a close thing, though. We were on our way out of the competition after a second-minute goal by Anderton until the unlikely intervention of Michael Ricketts, who came on as a sub and scored a late, late equaliser. Of the three goals he scored for the club, that one was by far the most valuable, taking the game into extra time. Neither side could find another goal, the penalty lottery luck was with us for a second time and we were into the semi-finals of the League Cup.

Christmas was then upon us, and the festivities were enjoyed with no worries about having to return overseas this time. Boro played their Boxing Day fixture in Lancashire, drawing 2-2 with Blackburn Rovers thanks to a brace from Juninho-ho-ho. The last game of the year was at home to Manchester United. It drew the biggest crowd of the season (a sell-out, no less) but United went away with all the points after a 1-0 win.

The third round of the FA Cup saw the visit of Notts County to the Riverside, and they were duly knocked out by an own goal and a Zenden strike. The Dutchman was entering a rich vein of form, and the fans had dedicated a song to him which was just typically Teesside in its steely humour:

"There's only one Bolo Zenden, one Bolo Zenden, he used to be shite, but now he's alright, walking in a Zenden wonderland!"

In the league, there was a home win against Fulham on a wintery Wednesday night followed by another four-goal mauling by the Gooners in North London. A 3-3 draw with Leicester on Teesside was followed by a break in the league programme to deal with a run of FA and Carling Cup games. We would face Arsenal three times in a matter of weeks, with the two legs of the Carling Cup semi-final straddling the FA Cup fourth round tie. I don't think I was alone in making one of those cerebral bargains that football fans often make in their heads: I would take a place in the League Cup final in return for defeat in the other cup. It was surely our best chance of silverware.

As it turned out, that's exactly what happened. In the first leg of the league cup semi-final, Boro beat a somewhat weakened Arsenal team 1-0 with a well-worked goal for Juninho, who celebrated with a wacky little dance on the Highbury turf. The FA Cup match was another 4-1 smashing for us, but they had brought out the big Gunners for that match. We hoped Mr. Wenger would again rest his big players for the return leg of the Carling Cup, but he played a much stronger team in the second leg than the first. No matter, we still managed to beat them 2-1 thanks to a Zenden goal and an own goal by Reyes to progress to the final. Bolton Wanderers had seen off Aston Villa in their semi-final, so it was the team from the North West who we would face. We obviously fancied our chances, but many of us remembered fancying our chances against Leicester seven years ago. We all know how that one went.

Another hugely satisfying league win at Leeds United came on the last day of January, with Zenden, Job and Ricketts giving us a 3-0 win. Then, in typical bloody Boro fashion, we lost 1-0 at home to Blackburn before going to Old Trafford and beating Manchester United 3-2. Juninho once again ran the show, scoring two goals (including a near-post header from the shortest player on the pitch). At 2-2 it looked like United were the natural choice to win, but Joseph Job had other ideas, spanking home a beauty from the edge of area to send the visiting contingent from Teesside into raptures. The last league game of the month was a defeat at St. James' Park by the Geordies. Ho hum.

And so it was upon us: The League Cup, or, to give it its sponsor's name, the Carling Cup Final. Could it happen this time? Could 128 years of hurt finally come to an end? The portents were good, not least in the fact that we would be playing at the Millennium Stadium in Cardiff rather than Wembley, which was still undergoing complete and very expensive reconstruction. There was also the date of the game: the leap year extra day of 29th February. It was a rare date, and maybe something rare would happen.

I managed to get myself a ticket, having made the prudent decision to buy a season ticket halfway through the season and thus improve my chances if we'd got there. There was a decent allocation for real fans at League Cup finals in Cardiff. I think both sets of fans were allocated nearly 30,000 tickets, so a good number got to go to the match. I'm sure there were those who were unlucky or who just couldn't make it at all, and I believe Bolton had some problems with their allocations. Such is life with cup finals. They are logistical challenges given the short time scales that are often at play; there's no doubt of that.

In the weeks leading up to the game I had been asked if I wanted to go to a BBC Radio 5 Live fans' forum being held on a midweek night at a pub in Bolton, so I joined about a dozen other people who ran, contributed to or posted on FMTTM's messageboard, including the likes of Rob Nichols and the legend they call Uncle Harry. We made our way over the Pennines with a "pies and peace" offering of some local pork products and found the venue. It was a large, modern pub with a cavernous open area. A group of tables was set up at one end of the room where the presenter, Jonathan Pearce, took up his central hosting position between Mark Lawrenson, Craig Hignett, Stan Collymore and Bolton legend, John McGinlay. In front of them were several rows of chairs seating Bolton fans. The small Boro contingent was ushered upstairs to a mezzanine area overlooking the main floor.

The show was lively and the banter was good-spirited. There was a roving reporter called Clem (himself a Teessider) who mingled with the fans when prompted, asking various questions and wandering around with the obligatory large microphone and headphones worn on one ear. During one such walkabout, Clem came towards me and thrust the microphone under my mouth, asking who I most feared from Bolton. My first, instinctive answer of "Peter Kay" raised a laugh in the crowd, although Mr. Pearce didn't look too impressed down on the main floor, but I soon gave a real answer and named Kevin Davies as someone who would definitely cause us problems in the game. He had been a thorn in our sides before, and I knew he was the kind of player defenders hate to face: a big, bustling nuisance who doesn't know the meaning of a lost cause.

After the show we found out that the actual League Cup trophy was there (it could have been a replica, of course, but it looked real enough) and a few of us had our photos taken gurning over the trophy with thumbs aloft and so on. Craig Hignett, ex-member of the dynamic strike duo of 1995-96 named the Midget Gems (partnered by Nick Barmby), came and chatted with us for a while and posed for more photos. A few drinks were imbibed and it was soon time to head back to the North East.

For the match itself, I decided to head down the night before the match and stay in a Travelodge just off the M4. This meant I could get into Cardiff nice and early without worrying about driving a long way twice in a day, especially as the weather had turned wintry. I gave another couple of Boro fans a lift down as well, and they stayed at the same hotel. Next morning we ate a hearty breakfast in the Little Chef next door and headed into Welsh Wales. I had never been to Wales in my entire life, and hoped I wouldn't be accosted by enormous unintelligible signs emblazoned with thirty-letter place names (made up of the letters H, L and U, mostly). It wasn't like that at all, of course, and it didn't take long to cross the Severn and get to Cardiff.

We were directed to car parks on the outskirts of the Welsh capital city, from where we could catch buses to the city centre. It was all fairly well organised and we got into the heart of the city with a good few hours to spare, and found that it was already buzzing with football fans. The strange thing was that it seemed to be all Boro. There were very few Bolton fans to be found, and all the pubs were awash with the reds and whites of Middlesbrough. There was a convivial and excited party atmosphere all around.

I headed to the Cardiff branch of the British Legion where a few people I knew where going to be meeting up for a few drinks. When I got there I found that they had a German beer called Bitburger which I hadn't tasted since I was a young slip of a lad back in the late 1980s. My excitement abated a tad when I found out that it was an alcohol-free version, but I still drank it. I was high enough on expectation as it was, and had to drive home after the game anyway.

Everyone was itching to get to the match, and there was an amazing feeling of optimism amongst the Boro fans. It was more optimistic than the feeling I'd witnessed back in 1997. It wasn't just optimism, actually, it was *belief*. This was our time, and I don't think we'd ever felt so sure of it. As kick-off time approached people finished their drinks, exchanged handshakes, hugs and back-pats and headed towards the venue for the cup final.

The Millennium stadium is an impressive venue, with high, white steel columns in each corner and polished black cladding around the top of the stands. On the day of our final it had Carling Cup banners draped from various structures. I made my way into the ground and up to my seat, which was high up at the back of one of the end stands. The retractable roof was closed for the match, and from the roof hung two huge banners bearing the club crests of Bolton and Boro. The centre circle was covered with a huge circle of cloth bearing the name of the sponsors. The stands were soon full of hopeful fans, decked out in their red and white shirts, hats and scarves and waving their flags. The atmosphere was crackling with expectancy and nails were bitten as news of the team selections came through. Hopes and dreams by the thousand were ready to pour out onto the pitch when the teams appeared.

The teams emerged a few minutes before kick-off to a background of vivid, moving colour and colossal noise. Fireworks erupted from the pitch and flash-bulbs by the thousand lit up the stands. The two teams lined up along the pitch, one on each side of the half-way line and did all the pre-match presentation stuff they like to torture us all with. Get on with it, will ya?

When it did start, it started better than anyone could have dared to imagine. In only the second minute Danny Mills knocked a long ball forward from right back. It was headed back into midfield where Mendieta suddenly had acres of space. He curled a gorgeous ball out to Zenden on the left wing, and Zenden whipped a wicked low cross into the six-yard box where Job slammed it home to give Boro the lead.

If that was good, better was to follow. French World Cup winner Djorkaeff had a chance for Bolton, saved well by Schwarzer to his right, and from the resulting corner Boro won a free kick for Bolton naughtiness in the area. A bit of head tennis ensued before Mendieta slid the ball in towards Job who was lurking in the area with his back to goal. As he tried to take the ball to one side, he was floored by a clumsy tackle from behind and referee Mr. Riley pointed to the spot. Oh. My. God. We had a penalty.

Zenden took the responsibility on his shoulders and stepped up to take the penalty kick. As he kicked his standing foot slipped and he did actually strike the ball twice, but the contacts were so close together it was only visible on a slow-mo replay, and the ball ended up in the net. Only six minutes had passed, and the Boro fans could barely contain themselves. I found myself hugging the bloke next to me, who I'd never seen before and have never seen since. I would have apologised, but he was hugging back with great enthusiasm.

On 21 minutes Bolton woke from their stunned stupor and hit back. It was a goal out of nothing by Kevin Bloody Davies (didn't I warn them?) with a weak, long-range shot from wide on the right. Schwarzer made a bit of a boo-boo of it, misjudging the bounce and letting the ball in at his near post. He was visibly annoyed by the mistake, kicking the goalpost in frustration. Of course Bolton came at us hard after that. They launched a series of attacks in their usual, Big-Sam-drilled way, but we stood firm. Schwarzer was a man possessed, making a series of great saves to quell the white-shirted hordes, and we made it to half time with the lead intact.

The second half wasn't half as hairy for Boro as it could have been. Bolton soon ran out of steam. They kept pressing for the equaliser, but Boro kept breaking quickly, and could well have scored a couple of goals up at the end of the ground where our nervous fans were seated. Mendieta had a couple of good chances and Juninho made a couple of trademark mazy runs, but the third goal wouldn't come. Ricketts came on for a bumbling cameo and our nerves were shot. Regulation time ran out and Bolton had four minutes of injury time to try and draw level. They threw everything forward, and there was a horrible, heart-in-the-mouth moment when Ehiogu's arm was struck by a goal-bound shot as he lunged across to block it from almost point-blank range. Mike Riley waved play on and we were so, so close to Paradise. The strains of "We Shall Overcome", that protest song of the civil rights movement adopted as an anthem of valiant defeat by Boro fans in the past, wasn't going to get an airing today. Please God, I can't say I really believe in you, but please: not today.

The roar at the final whistle was like nothing I've heard before or since. The release was immeasurable. Finally, finally, Middlesbrough had won a real trophy. Mickey Mouse trophy my arse. I stood with arms aloft and screamed until my lungs burned and my head span, then had to sit down to get my breath back. It was then that I wept like a big bloody baby, and I'm not ashamed to admit it. I'd not been a Boro fan for very long compared to many of those around me, but at that moment I felt 100% Teessider.

I'd seen cup final defeats and relegations, and this was sweeter and more *real* than anything I'd ever felt as a football fan, even in my foolish and misguided younger years. I can't imagine a Manchester United or Chelsea fan knowing how this moment feels. They win trophies all the time, so they get used to it. Hard times for them are going a season without winning a pot, whilst the majority of clubs just want to survive and go on the odd cup run, hoping to get a few crumbs thrown their way now and again by Sky Television.

The celebrations were long, lusty and loud. Long after the Bolton fans had vacated their half of the stadium to trudge home feeling hard done by (been there, done that), the stadium rocked to the Boro rhythm. The players partied on the pitch as much the fans did in the stands, with a beaming Juninho laying the ghosts of Elland Road to rest. You could see it meant a lot to him. I rang my parents on my mobile, giving them a replay of my full-time roar, but with all the noise around me, I wasn't sure who I was actually speaking to. It could well have been the answering machine.

The spectacular trophy presentation ceremony saw Gareth Southgate lift that glittering piece of silverware high above his head as fireworks shot towards the dark voids of the roof. Steve Gibson, the lad who came from the tough, working-class Middlesbrough estate of Park End to become one of the most popular chairmen in the modern game, was persuaded to come up to the podium and was lifted shoulder-high by the players. As for Steve McClaren, he hadn't been universally popular with fans of the club, but he had done the one thing no other manager had managed before: won a cup.

It was all just flipping fantastic, and I am so glad and I feel so privileged that I was there to see history being made.

We left the stadium in dribs and drabs and filtered back to our buses, trains and cars. For those on the roads, the drive home was long and slow, with horrendous traffic on the M4, but nobody in a red shirt gave a fig, quite honestly. We listened to the sports reports and plaudits on national radio and lapped it up. It was agreed that this had been one of the better cup finals of recent years. So many of the so-called dream finals featuring the big teams end up as stiff and stilted affairs. It was good to see two less fashionable clubs put on a good show, even if there could only be one winner. But, like I said, it was our time. It had been long, long overdue.

Naturally, the town of Middlesbrough was buzzing. The internet forums were flooded with people telling their own stories of the greatest weekend of their footballing lives. National newspapers were greedily devoured to get as many views as possible. I bought about half a dozen, even those I wouldn't normally use to eat my fish and chips off. We were finally getting positive press, with praise heaped on Gibson especially. The prospect of playing in next season's UEFA cup filled everyone with eager anticipation. Boro would be playing against some legendary teams in some far-flung, exotic destinations, and fans of these clubs would be visiting the Riverside. We couldn't wait.

I was even more delighted to find out when I got home that my wife had used the camcorder to record a bit of the final TV footage with my young son dancing around in front of the TV in full Boro kit, singing, "We've won the cup! We've won the cup!" The boy was learning, and best of all, was supporting a team that had now won something.

We got to thank the team a week or so later when they paraded the precious new trophy through the streets of Middlesbrough, starting near the site of Ayresome Park (now a housing estate) and finishing at the Riverside, reflecting the journey the club had taken in just a few years. I took my wife and son up to watch the start of the parade and got a few snaps of the jubilant players holding the trophy atop the open-topped double-decker bus.

Of course there was a Premier League season to finish off, with thirteen games left to play. It was no real surprise when the next of those games, away to Birmingham on the following Wednesday night, was lost 3-1. Most of the fans forgave that one, I think.

Four more games were played in March, with wins coming against Tottenham and Birmingham at home, a narrow defeat down at Charlton and a 1-1 draw with Everton. The home game with Birmingham was a quite memorable affair, featuring gale-force winds and the sharing of eight goals; six of those before half-time. Maccarone made a rare appearance and scored two of the goals.

Into April we went and Bolton came to the Riverside to have the cup final defeat rubbed in with a 2-0 beating before we drew 0-0 at Stamford Bridge. Southampton came next at home and were beaten 3-1 thanks to Juninho, Nemeth and Maccarone, and then we lost two games in a row to two teams from the Midlands: 2-0 away at Wolves and 2-1 at home to Aston Villa.

The season petered out somewhat as Boro lost away to Liverpool, beat Manchester City 2-1 at home and then gave a really poor showing down in Portsmouth on the last day of the season, losing 5-1. Boro finished eleventh in the table that season, which was solid, if unspectacular in league terms. Arsenal won the league and, just a few seasons after competing in the Champions League, Leeds United were relegated along with Leicester City and the Wandering Wolves. But that didn't matter. The hex on the club from Teesside was gone, the curses had been broken and history had been made. Now that European qualification had been secured, there were new and exciting times ahead.

There were exciting times ahead for my family as well. A couple of weeks after the end of the season our family size increased from three to four with the arrival of our daughter on 1st June 2004. She had been conceived in a world where Boro had never won a thing, but was born into a brave new, triumphant world of Boro success.

Chapter 12 - 2004/5

Just A Small Town In Europe

Looking back, 2004 was a pretty nasty year in terms of recent human history. There were the Madrid train bombings and that awful yet awesome display of nature's power with the tsunami that hit many parts of South East Asia on Boxing Day. We also had the re-election of George Dubya Bush, despite most people figuring out (and governments pretty much admitting) that the WMD danger in Iraq was non-existent. Blair met Colonel Gadaffi after the latter decided to stop acting like such an arse...for the time being.

The world of entertainment offered little in the way of welcome distraction, with the likes of Usher, Avril Lavigne and Norah Jones dominating the music scene, whilst *Shrek 2* and the face-clawingly bad *The Day After Tomorrow* dominated the box office charts.

In Sport we saw the Greeks triumphing at Euro 2004, before watching the summer Olympics taking place in Athens. Lance Armstrong won a sixth straight TDF and The Federernator won three out of four tennis Grand Slam tournaments.

I've already written about how 2004 had been a good year for Boro as well as for me and my family. The summer had seen our new daughter arrive on the scene, and after the success in the Carling Cup and European qualification, Boro saw the arrival of some real quality in the striking department. Mark Viduka joined from relegated Leeds United and Jimmy Floyd Hasselbaink was signed on a free transfer from Chelsea. Another Dutchman, Michael Reiziger, was signed from Barcelona on a "Bosman". Clog, cheese and tulip sellers were going to become busier on Teesside.

So everything was geared up for one of the most exciting seasons in the club's long history. There was a first knock-out, two-legged round to negotiate in the UEFA cup but, assuming we could negotiate it successfully, there would be a five-team mini-league where we would play two home games and two away games, playing each team once. It was a faint facsimile of the league structure that had been imposed on the European Cup when it became the Champions' League. All with a view to maximising revenue, I'm sure.

The league season opener was a game at home against those lovely black and white-festooned folk from up the A19, otherwise known as Newcastle United. As ever, sections of their fans entertained themselves by making reference to the child abuse scandal that caused so much distress in the Teesside area in the 1980s. Aren't they lovely? Still, we had the last laugh, with Hasselbaink scoring a cheekily blatant hand-balled goal late on to give us a 2-2 draw.

A quite astonishing game followed at Highbury against Arsenal, those French fancy Dans who just loved to give our defence the run-around. I watched it on TV and couldn't quite believe it when we went into a 3-1 lead, thanks to goals from Job, Jimmy and Franck Queudrue. This only spurred the Gooners on, however, and they stormed back to win 5-3 in the end, inspired by the ever-mercurial Denis Bergkamp. Another visit to the capital on the following Wednesday night gave us a first goal from Aussie Mark Viduka in a 2-0 win against Fulham.

Crystal Palace were up next (there are a LOT of teams from London, no?) and we beat them 2-1, with another goal from the new hero of the new Holgate, Mr. Hasselbaink. Viduka then rose to the challenge with a brace against Birmingham in the next home game. These chaps were no spring chickens, but they still did what they did very well, i.e. put the ball into the net. Five games in, we were in fourth place in the league, and dreaming of another stint in Europe before we'd even kicked a ball in our first campaign there.

The wait was soon to be over, and Boro would play their first game in Europe against Banik Ostrava from the Czech Republic on Thursday 16th September 2004. It was a special moment, but I'm sad to say I remember little about it. That afternoon I had been to the Friarage Hospital in Northallerton to have my upper wisdom teeth removed. I did watch the match on Channel 5, or whatever channel it had been grudgingly squeezed onto, but I was out of it on Co-codamol. Good stuff it is. So was the result, as it turns out, with a comfortable 3-0 win secured to take into the second leg. We were firm favourites to qualify for the league stage, and one of the better things about this new experience was seeing the antics of Eastern European fans, who performed strange, bare-chested routines with balloons in their little corner of the East stand.

The next two league games were lost 1-0, away to Everton and at home to Chelsea. It's tempting to say there was a Euro-hangover to blame, but that would be churlish. We didn't want to whinge about these things because we were playing in the UEFA Cup and having a great time. OK, we wanted to whinge a little bit. We had sunk to tenth in the league by this point after all.

The second leg of the Banik Ostrava tie was played in the Czech Republic at the end of September. It was preceded by a stream of people popping up on various internet forums enquiring as to the availability of cash machines and fast food outlets in Ostrava. Said people were assured that even if there weren't any golden arches, there would be plenty of cheap women and good-looking beer. This travelling-to-far-flung-former-Communist-countries-for-a-game-of-football lark was all very new to Boro fans.

In the game itself a goal from youngster James Morrison secured a 1-1 draw and qualification for the league stage. Boro fans behaved themselves in Ostrava and everyone was happy. We couldn't wait to see who we'd be drawn against next, and when the draw was made, we found ourselves in Group E, being rewarded with home games with Lazio and Partizan Belgrade and away games at Villareal and Egaleo. Everyone had confidence that we could progress to the round of thirty-two.

October started with a visit to Old Trafford in the Premier League. McClaren was building quite a good record against his old boss, Ferguson, and Boro came away with a creditable 1-1 draw featuring a goal by Stewie Downing. Another visit to the North West followed after the international break and JFH gave a virtuoso display of marksmanship, scoring a hat-trick in a 4-0 win over Blackburn Rovers. George Boateng got the other goal, his first for the club.

Next up was the first group-stage game in the UEFA cup, which meant a visit to Greece to play Egaleo. A handful of hardy souls took that trip and watched Boro win 1-0 with another goal from left winger Downing. Downing scored again in the next game, a home league fixture against Portsmouth, helping us rescue a point after falling behind.

By virtue of being in the UEFA Cup, Boro were given a pass straight into the third round of the league cup, which they were defending as champions, of course. I had decided that the time was right for me to take my son to a match. He was four years old now and enjoyed watching games on the telly, and I guessed that a low-key match with a small crowd would be a nice, gentle introduction to the live football experience. We were part of a very low crowd that night, with fewer than 12,000 people attending the match. Holding my hand very tightly, he looked absolutely enthralled by everything he saw as we approached the ground, entered through the turnstiles and climbed the stairs to take our seats. The game was won 3-0, but boyo missed the second half after curling up and falling asleep on his seat next to me. It was well past his bedtime when we got home, but I think he enjoyed it.

We then enjoyed seeing the team start a decent run in the league. We beat Charlton Athletic at the Valley with an own goal and a lovely little dinked goal by Bolo Zenden. This win took us back up to fourth position, and with ten games gone and the league taking shape, Boro fans were getting confident that this team could really go places. A top four finish was within our grasp if we could keep this up.

The first game of November was the UEFA cup home tie against the Italian Serie A team, Lazio. This was seen as a real challenge and would act as a means of measuring our progress. I went with an old mate from work and we sat and watched Middlesbrough take the Italians apart in front of a near-capacity crowd. Zenden scored an absolute peach of a goal in the first half before adding another in the second to give us a 2-0 win. The Riverside was rocking. Belief was rocketing. We were heading into uncharted waters.

A niggle-filled game against Bolton followed at the weekend, but we snatched a draw with a late Boateng goal, before moving on to the business of attempting to defend our League Cup trophy against Liverpool at Anfield. It didn't end well, despite holding out for most of the game. Two late goals did for us and we were out.

No matter, the league was still bearing fruit. There was a televised game against our former manager's West Brom side at the Hawthorns the following weekend, and I remember it being a pretty dour game and performance, which we somehow managed to win 2-1. We again had to thank Zenden and Own Goal for scoring, but we also had to thank Kanu – a man who had tortured us more than once in an Arsenal shirt – for missing from about a yard out. How he managed it is anyone's guess. Bryan Robson didn't look impressed. Next up was Liverpool at home, and Zenden was again in the goals along with

Chris Riggott to give us a 2-0 win. We were still fourth in the league, and all was blooming and smelling lovely in the garden.

Then came a tough away game in the UEFA Cup, with a visit to Villareal in late November. They had Champions League pedigree and were obviously a tough proposition in front of their own crowd. Large numbers of Boro fans travelled with the team this time, hoping to absorb some local culture and sample some local beverages. At the match, they saw the team being given a bit of a lesson by Villareal, and it could have been worse than 2-0 in the end.

No matter, these lessons are all part of the experience, and we take them on board and move on. We only had to finish in the top three of our group to qualify, so it wasn't a disaster by any means.

Tottenham decided to join in on providing lessons and also beat us 2-0 in the next Premiership match. Were these European trips taking it out of us? Maybe; maybe not, but we definitely seemed to be playing badly and/or not winning after the UEFA Cup away games. Our two new star strikers had gone a bit quiet on us as well, with neither having scored since the game at Blackburn back in mid-October. The bright side was that we were still in fifth position, which would gain us a place back in the UEFA Cup if we managed to stay there.

Viduka and Hasselbaink decided to put things right in the next home match on a Monday night in early December, sharing the goals in a 3-2 win over Manchester City. Man City were left feeling somewhat aggrieved when a perfectly good goal was disallowed for offside. Along with the number of own goals going in for us, it did seem that Lady Luck was giving us a little helping hand this season. Some say you make your own luck, but I don't know, because I've never seen a Luck kit in any Airfix model shop that I've been in, and I don't have a clue what the raw materials are...

OG scored yet another goal along with Downing to give us a 2-2 draw at Southampton and then we were playing the last match of the group stage in the UEFA Cup. A much-reduced crowd saw a much-rotated team beat Partizan of Belgrade by 3 goals to 0, with goals from Job, Nemeth and Morrison. We were into the last 32, and were drawn to play the Austrian Red Devils, aka Grazer AK.

With 2004 rapidly running out of days, we finally won a home league game against Aston Villa. Michael Reiziger scored a good goal and Jimmy Floyd and Joseph Job got the others, but the game was notable for the way Boro played, i.e. not very well. Martin O'Neill was completely flabbergasted at the result, but Boro fans were quite happy to see that the team could win in such a manner. Having quality where it counts makes a huge difference to any team.

Christmas came along, and everyone got fat and possibly a bit merry. Boro went to Birmingham on Boxing Day and got stuffed like a dead bird. If 2-0 counts as a stuffing, that is. We made amends two days later by beating Norwich City 2-0 at home. 2004 finished with Boro looking good in the Premier League and with more European football on the horizon. With the trophy win in February, it was going to take something special for this year to be surpassed.

2005 Started with a 2-0 home reverse to Manchester United, followed by a defeat by the same scoreline away at Chelsea. The good old post-Christmas slump seemed to be taking hold, and we slipped to sixth in the table, which was still a European qualifying spot. We did manage to get through the third round of the FA Cup with a 2-1 win at Notts County thanks to Job and Brazilian midfield warhorse Doriva. The next league match was a 1-1 draw against Everton at home, virtue of a Joseph Job goal. It wasn't a bad result given that Everton were also near the business end of the table and also looking to qualify for a European competition.

The following game was memorable for almost comical reasons. We faced Norwich down at Carrow Road, and after the even-Stevens first half ended 1-1, Boro took control. Two goals apiece from JFH and French Franck gave us what should have been an unassailable 4-1 lead. Somehow Norwich clawed their way back into the match and managed to get back to 4-4. It's a good job the full time whistle was blown by the ref just after their fourth, because they could and probably would have gone on to get a winning fifth, such was the way the momentum had swung to their side. January ended with an ignominious exit from the FA Cup with a 3-0 defeat at Old Trafford.

February began with dreadful away defeat down in Portsmouth, but there was at least some relief when we managed to beat Blackburn at home, 1-0. A no-score draw at Bolton's Reebok stadium kept the points tally ticking over, and kept us in sixth, but there was some dismay at the way the team had started the New Year. There had been only one win since the strains of Auld Lang Syne had echoed away into the ether. At least we still had the UEFA Cup to compete in, and the next game up was the two-legged round of 32 tie against the Austrians.

The away leg in Graz saw a hard-fought match finish 2-2 with strikes by Zenden and Hasselbaink. Exactly a week later they came to the Riverside for the second leg and were seen off 2-1, with goals by Morrison and JFH. Everyone was hoping that Jimmy would find his scoring touch in the league once again.

A year on from the triumph in Cardiff, Boro finished February with a 2-2 draw at home with Charlton Athletic. Chris Riggott and Danny Graham scored the goals. The less-than-impressive league form continued with a 2-0 away defeat at Villa, and we sunk out of the top six for the first time since October.

A difficult task then faced Middlesbrough in the last 16 of the UEFA Cup. Sporting Lisbon stood between us and progress to the quarter finals. On an early March evening, a crowd of only around 23,000 turned up to watch Boro being given another lesson in the harsh realities of European football. Lisbon went into a 3-0 lead after half-time, and it looked like the game was up. The adventure looked to be over, for this season at least. Even a spectacular long-range scissor-kick volley by Job and a goal by Riggott did little to lift the mood. The crowd size caused had people wondering if the fans were becoming disillusioned with the team again, or if they were just flat out of cash having followed the team all around Europe.

Maybe they were just saving up for the trip to Portugal. The following week there were some legendary shenanigans in the fountains of Lisbon, and the young team put up a hell of a fight, but were beaten 1-0 on the night and 4-2 on aggregate. Dream Over. Please enter more hope and dreams to continue. We had to start winning again and get back up that league so we could get back into the qualification spots. The European exploits had been fun, and there most definitely *was* an appetite for more.

So much for that sentiment. We promptly went and lost 3-1 at home to Southampton and found ourselves down in ninth position. April started well with a 1-0 away win at Selhurst Park against the Palace of Crystal. Frank Queudrue once again proved his worth as an attacking-minded full-back, grabbing the winner. We then had a sequence of three home games were we hoped to pick up some much-needed points. Arsenal only beat us by the single goal for once, and following a 1-1 draw with Fulham we found our form again against West Bromwich Albion, giving them a 4-0 spanking. Szilard Nemeth, in for the long-term injured Viduka, scored two of them to show Jimmy and Mark that were actually other strikers capable of staking a claim and scoring a bloody goal or two.

The other two games of the Easter schedule saw a 0-0 draw away at Newcastle followed by a 1-1 draw against Liverpool at Anfield, with Nemeth again on the scoresheet. Boro were back up to seventh place and in with a chance of getting back into Europe, especially now that there was an extra place in the UEFA Cup up for grabs thanks to one of the top four teams actually taking it seriously and winning the League Cup. The last home game, in front of a near sell-out crowd, saw Tottenham beaten 1-0 with a goal by General George Boateng, and we were suddenly headed for a crunch game with Stuart Pearce's Manchester City. It was us or them, and we only needed a point to pip them to seventh place and European qualification.

On Sunday 15th May, Boro went to the City of Manchester Stadium with their destiny squarely in their own hands. It turned out one huge pair of gloved hands would make the difference.

In the 23rd minute Jimmy lined up a free kick from thirty yards out. He showed that he still knew where the goal was with a stupidly hard, arcing shot that rattled in off the bar, leaving David James grasping thin air. Get in. City fought back, as expected, and drew level early in the second half through Musampa. They knocked hard at the door all the way through the second half, but Boro held firm, with Southgate and Ehiogu doing everything they possibly could to stop them scoring. The game was into injury time when referee Rob Styles spotted a handball by Franck Queudrue and pointed to the spot. Oh, bugger.

It was all down to one kick. Robbie Fowler stepped up to strike, and big Mark Schwarzer made one of the most important penalty saves he's ever made to deny him. Boro fans in the stadium and all around the world erupted as they heard Ali Brownlee shouting something about the biggest Aussie hero since Ned Kelly. We were back in Europe, this time via the league. Given the way the team had played since the turn of the year, winning only four games in the league, it was really quite something; magnificent, in fact.

And that was that. Chelsea bought the league title with their Russian roubles and Southampton went down with Norwich and Palace. Boro had another UEFA Cup campaign to plan for and had finished in their highest ever Premier League position. Some fans – those who are never blooming satisfied – whined and bitched about how it could have been even better, but in terms of Boro's history, it was going to take something special to surpass.

In my little life, things were just bumbling along nicely. I was working in freelance roles around North Yorkshire and Humberside and trying to keep my head above the tide of bills, dirty nappies and cuddly toys at home. All good fun, really. I still got the occasional Boro match, but my main way to let off steam was playing online games like *Rainbow Six* and *Pro Evolution Soccer 4* on my Xbox. There's nothing like screaming abuse at American teenagers with Jedi-like reactions to get the juices flowing at 2am in the morning. It also gets the wife a bit excited, I find, although not in a good way.

One game I really liked playing around that time was *Medal of Honour Frontline*. It is actually one of my favourite video games of all time. It was visceral, realistic and had an amazing soundtrack, plunging the player into the events following the D-Day landings and fighting the Nazi occupiers back through France and the Netherlands. It featured battles from *Operation Market Garden*, including the bridge at Nijmegen, which the player has to cross to get to Arnhem. Anyone who has seen war films like *A Bridge Too Far* would have heard these names, and they would once more ring bells with me and other Boro fans within a matter of months.

Chapter 13 - 2005/06

A Dream Too Far

In the year of our Lord 2005, the world witnessed some quite significant moments. Pope John Paul II died, home-grown Islamic extremists caused murder and mayhem in London on 7th July and Hurricane Katrina brought death and destruction to New Orleans. Those of faith must have been wondering where their Lord was and what the heck he was thinking.

The music and films of the year were unremarkable in the main, with the likes of Mariah Carey and Kelly Clarkson in the charts and the box office dominated by remakes and sequels. There was another *Harry Potter* film about a goblet or something, the third and best of the *Star Wars* prequels and Speilberg's odd attempt to bring HG Wells' classic *War of the Worlds* up to date.

In the wider world of sport, Liverpool won the Champions' League Final in Istanbul, coming back from 3-0 down to AC Milan at half-time. I expect them to still be going on about it in 2205. Lance won his seventh straight cycle race in the land of legless frogs and England's Test cricket side won a superb Ashes series, sending Warney and co. back down under with their marsupial tails between their legs.

As for Boro, they had another season in Europe to look forward to, and invested in more firepower for the forward line, signing the Nigerian Yakubu from Portsmouth for the tidy sum of £7.5 million. Our appetite for Brazilian midfielders was once again fed when Fabio Rochemback was signed from Barcelona, although he had been on long-term loan with Sporting Club de Portugal (or Sporting Lisbon as they are known to most). The other signing of note was one Emmanuel Pogatetz, a man with a fearsome reputation who had been on loan to Spartak Moscow when he broke an opponent's leg and ended up serving a lengthy ban.

The league campaign started inauspiciously enough with a 0-0 draw at home to Liverpool and a 2-0 defeat away at Spurs. The team eventually got going with a good 3-0 win over the Birmingham boys in blue at the Riverside, with a couple of goals by Mr. Viduka. August didn't end well, however. Charlton Athletic came to Middlesbrough and dished up a humiliating 3-0 home defeat. The international break was probably coming at a good time, especially with the ominous shape of Arsenal coming up next at the Riverside.

In an occurrence rarer than a night on the town ending without seeing at least one fight and a discarded parmo, Boro actually beat Arsene's Arsenal 2-1 at the Riverside. Yakubu got his first and Massimo Maccarone, the forgotten 8.15 million quid man who had spent the previous season on loan at various clubs in Italy, got the other.

Thoughts then turned back to the UEFA Cup. Standing between Boro and the group stages this time were the Greek outfit, Xanthi. This early game didn't attract a very big crowd with fewer than 15,000 there to watch Boateng and Viduka give us a nice 2-0 lead to take to the North East of Greece.

The stuttering start to the Premiership schedule continued through September with a 1-1 draw at the capital of piers and pies, Wigan. The Mackems then came to our patch and won 2-0. This start to the season was not very inspiring at all. We were sitting in eleventh place after seven games. No matter, we had different, if not more sizeable, sharks to sauté, and the second leg of the UEFA Cup first round tie in Greece came around. Boro went and secured their progress with a 0-0 draw.

Next up in the league, at the beginning of October, we visited Aston Villa at Villa Park. The Yak, as our new muscular Nigerian had come to be known, scored two and Villa old boy George Boateng got the other in a satisfying and rare win in Birmingham. Yakubu then showed a desire to score against his old club in a 1-1 draw with Portsmouth at home.

The UEFA Cup schedule resumed and Boro were to face Grasshoppers of Zurich in their first group game. The game was away in the land of chocolate and cuckoo clocks, but Boro came away with a vital win thanks to a single goal by Jimmy Floyd Hasselbaink, scoring his first of the season.

Next up was a league game down in the East End of London against West Ham. It's never a happy hunting ground down there, and they do have some odious elements within their support. Combining this with the extraordinary, almost sneering, sense of entitlement they seem to have at times (West Aam wan the Weld Cap, y'know!) , they don't really have many friends on Teesside. It was a 2-1 defeat for us this time, and ten games into the season we were showing all the dreadful hallmarks of a plodding mid-table side who couldn't find any consistency either way. There hadn't been two consecutive results the same as yet.

An away win at Everton in the third round of the League Cup lightened things a touch, but something really special and unprecedented was just around the corner. Home games against Manchester United tend to bring in big crowds, often capacity ones, but this time round it was still about 5,000 short of capacity. The game kicking off on a Saturday night for TV coverage may have had a little influence, but crowds had generally been in decline this season.

Those who didn't go may have regretted not doing so. I know I do, because Boro put on an amazing show to beat Manchester United 4-1. Yes, that's right. 4-1. Mendieta played the game of his life, starting this rout with a long-range shot that somehow bamboozled Edwin Van der Saar to give us an early lead. JFH made the most of a Ferdinand slip to make it 2-0, and then the Yak's penalty had Teesside pinching itself with the half-time score-line of 3-0. In the second half Mendieta got his second to make it 4-0 before Cristiano Ronaldo scored a late consolation effort. Of course, it was all down to United having an off day, not because Boro were just better on the day. I believe everything the mass media tell me, and that's that.

The low crowds were becoming a bit of a talking point for fans and pundits. The national media, bless their cotton socks, weren't shy in showing or writing about the growing areas of empty red seats at the Riverside. I wasn't getting to many matches myself for various reasons that I could expand on for a few paragraphs, but it's pretty pointless. I'm not here to tell anyone that I'm the best fan or the worst fan in the world. In a nutshell I was short on funds and had other priorities in my life.

I'm sure there were others who had similar problems, but I also think that this was the start of a general decline in football attendances that we are now seeing across the board. Prices were getting beginning to get quite steep for families attending the games. Adding the cost of transport, food and drink to the cost of the match ticket quickly made it quite an expensive undertaking, especially if it was done on a regular basis. Season ticket numbers had declined and now people were picking and choosing their games. There were potentially a lot of extra games to watch this season.

And so when only 13,000 turned up to watch Boro take on the Ukranian team, Dnipro in the second group match, it wasn't really a surprise. They weren't a particularly big name. I've never heard of them before or since, and guess that some people were waiting for potentially bigger teams later down the line. Of course some will point out that you go to watch Middlesbrough, not the opposition, but as I've said people were picking their games now, so they weren't going to plump for Dnipro if they could save their money for more glamorous opposition.

Ever willing and able to confound any hint of expectation, Boro went to play Everton at Goodison Park and lost 1-0, but beat Fulham at home 3-2 in the following game. Yakubu was scoring the main bulk of the goals, with JFH chipping in here and there. Viduka was proving to be injury prone this time round and didn't feature that heavily in the first half of the season.

Next up in the UEFA Cup was AZ Alkmaar in Holland. It was a potentially tricky tie played on a tight little ground on a wet and windy November night. Boro battled gamely to nick a 0-0 draw, but the game itself was overshadowed by the murder of a Boro fan in Amsterdam.

November was seen out with a 2-2 home draw with West Brom, Viduka made an appearance and scored one of the goals, and scored again in the midweek League Cup tie with Crystal Palace, which took us into the quarter finals.

Boro finally managed to find some consistency in early December; unfortunately it was the bad kind, and there were losses away to Chelsea and Liverpool, 1-0 and 2-0 respectively.

The final game of the group stages of the UEFA Cup featured an even smaller crowd than against Dnipro. This time an even more obscure team called Litex Lovech were the visitors, and fewer than 10,000 hardy souls parted with their cash and braved that mid-December night. They saw Boro beat the Bulgarians 2-0, thereby making progress into the next round. The UEFA cup was now on hold until February.

The last league game before Christmas saw a cracking 3-3 draw against Spurs at the Riverside, with the Yak adding two more goals to his tally. We found ourselves in the lower half of the league table and going into a period when Boro traditionally suffer a slump. The feeling that this slump could be a bad one wasn't helped when Blackburn beat us at home in the league cup quarter final thanks to a last-minute goal by veteran nuisance, Paul Dickov.

And so it was Christmas once more. My little family was on the move again to a different part of Thirsk and I was trying to find myself a more stable job, having spent a while on short-term freelance contracts in various parts of the North of England. There was some hope of a more permanent role up in Middlesbrough if I did well at an interview scheduled for the New Year.

Blackburn found Boro in generous spirits on Boxing Day, taking three points back to Lancashire with them thanks to a 2-0 win, which went nicely with the league cup win only five days earlier. 2005 was completed with a 0-0 draw against Manchester City.

2006 started with a decent result up in the land of the Deluded Penguins as Yakubu and Hasselbaink scored in a 2-2 draw. Next up was the FA Cup third round and Boro faced the prospect of being on the wrong end of an embarrassing giant-killing at non-league Nuneaton. We scrapped and scraped a 1-1 draw to earn a replay back up on Teesside. We lived to fight another day in the FA Cup.

In the league, Boro may well have wanted the ground to swallow them up in the next game. With six teenagers playing and with Doriva getting himself sent off, we were absolutely battered 7-0 by the Gooners. Thierry Henry scored a hat-trick, which is nice, and McClaren described the game as his toughest day so far.

The replay with Nuneaton was won 5-2, but the sheen from that was soon gone when Wigan came and beat us 3-2 on our patch in the league. We had slipped to seventeenth in the league and things were not looking promising at all.

At least my own life was brightening up. I got that job I was hoping for with the consultancy in Middlesbrough, and was glad to be back in familiar surroundings surrounded by people who said,

"Yerjokinarnyer?" at regular intervals. Football talk wasn't really high on the agenda around this time, for some reason.

Another FA Cup match was upon us, this time against Coventry in the fourth round. We would again end up taking the game to a replay virtue of a 1-1 draw. These fixtures were piling up quickly, and replays like this weren't helping matters.

Still, some joy was finally found in the league. Without a win since November, Boro went to Sunderland and beat them 3-0, with goals by Stuart Parnaby, Pogatetz and Jimmy the F to the H. The Mackems were having a terrible season, and Boro weren't in the mood to give them any comfort.

Villa were in no mood to give us any comfort when they visited Middlesbrough at the beginning of February. They spanked Boro 4-0, and the crowd gave vent to their dissatisfaction with the way things were going. One fan actually ran from his seat and flung his season ticket book towards Steve McClaren before being bundled away by stewards. It proved to be something of a watershed low point of the season. There was no intention or indeed desire to go lower than the seventeenth place currently being inhabited.

For me, my initial joy at getting a local job was short-lived. I soon found myself having to travel down to Reading on a secondment to a large American engineering firm whose offices are the size of a small town. There was a gym and a cash-machine, but there were no branches of McDonalds, should any European-bound Boro fans get a little lost on the M4 corridor. I didn't mind too much, as there were a few lads from the North East on the same secondment, and we would often go for meals and drinks together after work and talk about how rubbish it was down south.

The Coventry FA Cup replay was won 1-0 with a JFH goal, and then it was the turn of Chelsea to come up to the North East. Boro did what they did best; tearing up the form book and playing out of their skins against the so-called big team, and beat the Russian's playthings 3-0. Rochemback, Downing and Yakubu got the goals in what was Chelsea's heaviest defeat to date under Jose "I'm Special, Me" Mourinho. Once again, Boro fans were left scratching their heads at their team's ability to turn over teams like Chelsea and Manchester United but lose at home to Wigan.

For once, the team were able to take some of the buzz of a good win forward with them. They travelled to Germany to play a team called Verein für Bewegungsspiele Stuttgart 1893 e. V., which is more of a mouthful than a bratwurst, so they're more commonly known as VfB Stuttgart. Either way, the Germans didn't reckon for the silky skills of Stuart Parnaby, who joined Hasselbaink on the score sheet in a 2-1 away win in the first leg of this round of 32 tie. It was a remarkable result, really. I watched it in a Reading pub with a few of my colleagues. There weren't many other people watching the big screen in the side room we took over, which meant we were able to enjoy the game without suffering any wise-cracking Southerners making sarcastic remarks about smog monsters. I wouldn't have cared anyway, because the result was just brilliant.

Next up it was time for a visit to the North West to play the North End of Preston in the fifth round of the FA Cup. A fairly comfortable 2-0 win was secured with two more goals by Yakubu. We were in the quarter finals of the cup, and at least we didn't need a replay this time.

The return home leg of the Stuttgart tie was next, and a larger crowd turned out to watch a terrifying, edgy game which the Germans won 1-0 to level on aggregate. Boro were to benefit from that curiosity of European cup competitions, the away goal, and won the tie because of the two scored in Stuttgart. Super-dooper.

The team's and fans' spirits were definitely raised now, and Boro strung together two wins on the trot against teams from England's second city, beating West Brom 2-0 at the Hawthorns and Birmingham 1-0 at home. The league position was looking slightly better, with a climb away from the danger zone up to fifteenth.

The UEFA Cup games were coming thick and fast now, and I went along to my new local in Reading to watch Boro take on another potentially difficult team in the shape of Roma. It was a tense, tight affair, but Jimmy Floyd first earned then scored the winning penalty to give us the slenderest of advantages to take to the Stadio Olympico in Rome.

It was Charlton Athletic down at the Valley next in the league, a game that would act as a warm-up for the upcoming FA Cup quarter final match. This quirk seems to have happened a lot in the last few seasons, where we end up playing the same team two or three times in the space of a few weeks. At least it wasn't a four-game sequence against Arsenal this time. Charlton won this particular round 2-1. I think we probably had our eyes on the forthcoming trip to Rome, where we were hoping to make it to the quarter finals of the UEFA Cup as well.

The game in Rome will live long in the memory for those who saw it on TV, and even more so for those who travelled there to see it. By all accounts the treatment dished out to Boro fans by Italian police was nothing short of disgraceful, but the result more than made up for it. Boro took the lead through the sweetest of goals, with Hasselbaink rising to meet an exquisite cross by Downing and plant it past the Roma 'keeper. Roma had to score three times now. They battled and battered at the door, managing to score one just before half-time and then scoring from a penalty mid-way into the second half. Schwarzer was in the thick of the action, making some great saves, and when Mexes was sent off for Roma in the last minute, we felt that we were there. And so it proved.

Yes, we had ridden our luck a touch, but we had now beaten teams of real quality in Stuttgart and Roma to make it into the quarter finals. Absolutely excellent. The fans kept back in the stadium for hours had reason to be cheerful at least. They amused themselves with renditions of songs about being just a small town in Europe, and the new favourite terrace tune: "*Geordies at Home Watching the Bill*".

What was even more excellent was finishing my secondment down in Reading, which meant I could work back up in the Boro. I would be able to get to a game or two as well, now that I had a bit of disposable income. Well, that's what I told the wife, anyway.

Our league form suffered a European hangover once again and we lost 3-2 away to Blackburn. Thankfully our league position didn't slip too badly. There were too many bad teams below us trying to get into double figures...points wise. Still, there was the small matter of the FA Cup quarter final to attend to, and that meant another trip down to South London to play Charlton. The game ended in a rather dull 0-0 draw, and yet another match – the requisite replay - was added to the schedule. There was suddenly a smidgen - just a smidgen – of sympathy with the likes of Manchester United who argue that squads have to be rotated to survive in long, hard seasons where the games come thick and fast.

Of course, a high-as-possible finish in the Premiership was high on the list of priorities, and the next game was a tasty encounter at the Riverside with the visit of those Wandering types from Bolton. A pulsating, bruising encounter was eventually won 4-3 with a late goal by Parnaby, but there were some ugly scenes as nuisance-in-chief Kevin Davies caught Pogatetz with an elbow late in the match. It's always hard to say if there is any real intent, but the Pog was not amused at being made to bleed.

Right at the end of March Boro faced another stern test in the UEFA Cup quarter finals against FC Basle of Switzerland. The first leg was away, and the team took a good following with them to the Alpine wonderland (even if the city itself is actually located in the lowlands of Switzerland). Just before kick-off, the teams were greeted with a card display at one end of the ground showing a large tin-foil approximation of the UEFA Cup with beams of light radiating away from it. That was fair enough, but the message on the banner across the middle wasn't very polite or called for, to be honest. It read, in huge, yellow capital letters: BEAT THAT FUCKING BORO – WIN THE CUP TOMORROW. "Boro" doesn't even rhyme with "tomorrow", for flip's sake...

It may just have had some psychological effect. Basle won 2-0 quite easily, and could probably have had one or two more goals. Boro were pretty dreadful, but at least it was only half-time in the tie, and the home leg was to come. It wasn't all over just yet.

For once there were no ill-effects from the travelling, and in the league game against Man City, youngster Lee Cattermole scored the winner in a 1-0 win. Boro had now lifted themselves up to fourteenth position and were looking comfortable in mid-table.

Then it was time for that second leg against Basle. As I was living and working locally again, I decided it might be worth going along to see if we could pull ourselves back from 2-0 down. It should be entertaining on some level, I thought. It's a shame that many more didn't feel the same way. The crowd was just short of 25,000, but then I guess many thought the chances of coming back were slim. More fool them, eh?

The first half of the first half saw a spirited start by Boro, including a penalty appeal and a few shots on goal, but Basle decided to take the lead midway through the half with a simple tap-in for Eduardo. Boro now needed four goals to win. A tall order, if ever there was one.

Viduka pulled one back just before half time after breaking through the Swiss defence and McClaren then decided it was time to go for broke, taking Morrison off and putting on Hasselbaink to join Viduka and the Yak up front. Just as the hour-mark approached, big Aussie Mark scored another, sliding the ball home to make it 2-1 on the night. Belief was starting to build. The crowd made up for the 10,000 missing fans by creating a hell of a noise, willing the team on. McClaren then sent on forgotten man Maccarone to replace Franck Queudrue and Boro went for it, helped in part by the sending off of a Basle defender. In the 79th minute JFH found some space at the edge of the area and placed an exquisite, powerful shot into the top corner of the net. 3-3 on aggregate and there was only one way this was going.

Shot after shot rained down on the Basle goal, but their 'keeper blocked everything that came his way. Rochemback sent a couple of pile-drivers goalwards, but to no avail. Time was running out. In the last minute we were all desperately pleading for a miracle. Rochemback took another long-range shot which Zuberbuhler could only parry to his left. Maccarone came charging in onto the rebound and somehow managed to slide it into the net. Cue pandemonium. The comeback was complete and we were into the semi-finals.

I left the stadium that night unable to speak or even think straight. I'd never seen anything like that in my life. We had been 3-0 down with only an hour or so left to play, but had managed to rise from the ashes to perform an amazing feat. I got in my car and drove home to Thirsk, listening in silence to the amazed and delighted voices of fans calling in to talk to Ali and Bernie on the radio phone-in. We were in the semi-finals of the UEFA Cup, and standing between us and the final in Eindhoven were a club of real European pedigree: Steaua Bucharest.

It was a club of rather more mythical pedigree we were up against in the next league. Everyone's second favourite team, the eighth biggest team in the world, the sleeping giants...all those other fanciful titles given to the club (usually by their own fans) up the A19 who hadn't won a cup in half a century. Still, they did triumph on this occasion (bless 'em) winning 2-1 at the Riverside. It must have made them quite happy until they remembered how well that small town in

Yorkshire were doing in Europe whilst they sat at home watching police dramas.

In the other cup competition that we still had a stake in Boro had another replay to get through, this time against Charlton. It seemed aeons had passed since that first goalless draw, even though it was only around three weeks. Anyway, the game was an entertaining goal-fest, with Boro prevailing 4-2 in the end. Viduka's goal was a real peach, with the big man showing his undeniable skill with a series of twists and turns to bamboozle the Charlton defenders before blasting it into the net. So into the FA Cup semi-finals we marched and it was West Ham who we had to face for a place in the final. Chelsea and Liverpool were drawn in the other semi, which probably upset the sponsors, not to mention the Sky TV generation who only seem interested in a game if there are so-called "glamour" teams involved.

Another poor league performance followed with a 1-0 loss away at Pompey, but the league position held firm. The next home game, to West Ham, gave us hope that we could do the business in the FA Cup, as we won 2-0 quite comfortably. All was going swimmingly, and it was Bucharest up next.

A solid contingent of Boro fans again invaded foreign shores, this time to Romania, giving the locals of Bucharest a taste of Teesside craic. I've no doubt on or two Romanians had to field questions as to the whereabouts of the nearest Maccie D's. The game itself was a forgettable, sterile affair, won by a single goal by Dica or someone else sounding like the name of a record company. 1-0 away isn't a disaster, and even less of a mountain to negotiate than was presented in the quarter finals. We had to be confident that we could make it to the final in Eindhoven.

As if there weren't enough big games to negotiate, Boro then had to play West Ham in the FA Cup semi-final at the neutral venue of Villa Park. It was more expense for the travelling Boro faithful, but these days really were rare and just had to be enjoyed. I'm sure many people hunted down the back of sofas and raided their piggy banks to cough up for tickets. They probably wished they hadn't bothered for this one, to be fair. It was an ugly game, marred by the injury caused to Mark Schwarzer's cheekbone by Dean Ashton's elbow and ultimately won by a single goal scored by Marlon Harewood in the 77th minute.

Suddenly the mood on Teesside changed. One semi-final had been lost and we were down 1-0 in the other. It could end up as just another potless season to go with the other 129 or whatever the number was now. It would be pretty gutting to have got this far in two cup competitions and not even get to the final of one of them.

It was no surprise, then, when a capacity crowd turned up for the next game: the second leg of that UEFA Cup semi against Steaua Bucharest. This could well be the last big game of the season, and in terms of an occasion there had been no other like it at the Riverside. I managed to get a ticket for this one, taking my seat in the South stand where I got a great view of the card display organised by fans for the North stand. There were no obscenities here, simply the name of a Dutch town where we hoped to be playing a game on 10th May: Eindhoven. Some nay-sayers had criticised this as tempting fate, but it looked great. The crowd were up for it, even without the help of the laughable recorded chants of *"Come on Boro"* that were piped through the PA before and in the early stages of the game. The person was hopefully shamed into stopping this horribly naff behaviour. Gerrafuckinggrip, man!

As for the game, it started pretty terribly. Steaua found themselves 2-0 up in the game and 3-0 up on aggregate within 25 minutes thanks to two hesitant moments by Brad Jones, who was standing in for the injured Schwarzer. Oh bugger. The Steaua fans couldn't quite believe it, and one of them even charged onto the pitch after the second goal before passing out in the centre circle and being carted away. We were once again 3-0 down with only an hour or so to play. McClaren found his hand forced by injury to Gareth Southgate and sent Maccarone on after only 26 minutes, and it was a change that paid dividends quickly as the Italian latched onto a pass by Viduka and placed an angled shot into the net. Hope was rearing its fickle head once again. Could we really do the impossible again? Really?

A couple of chances were fluffed before the first half ended, and in the second the pressure built and built on the Romanian goal. Hasselbaink missed a chance by inches before Yakubu was thrown on to make it a four-man attack in the 55th minute, and in the 62nd minute a deep cross by Downing was headed into the Bucharest goal by Viduka. 2-3. Belief was battling to take hope's place now and the home fans scented blood. In the 72nd minute a long throw was only half-cleared to Downing, and his cross-shot was bundled over the line by Chris Riggott after being parried by the Steaua 'keeper.

Just less than twenty minutes were left to do it. Surely we could do it. In the stands we were beside ourselves and to a man, woman and child were willing the team to score the fourth goal. Once again, time was almost up when the Romanians fluffed another clearance, giving Downing the chance to skin his full-back and whip in a cross that was just crying out to be headed in. Who else but Maccarone obliged, diving full-length to get his shiny forehead onto the ball and plant it past the desperate dive of the goalie.

AAAAAAAAAAAAAAAAARRRRRRRRRRGGGGGGGGHHHH
HHHHHH!!!!!!

I think that's the sound that came from about 30,000 pairs of lungs in the Riverside at that moment. I nearly passed out, just as I nearly had at Cardiff. I know that a high-pitched girly version of this was heard over the airwaves of BBC Tees when the goal was scored, as Paul Addison (I think it was) screamed his delight at lightning striking twice. I've also heard that there were a fair few pubs up and down the country full of screaming, disbelieving people. Plenty of them weren't Boro fans, but had been captivated by this incredible match and another incredible comeback.

So lightning really had struck twice. Maccarone had again scored a fourth goal in the last minute to overturn a 3-0 deficit. The odds on this happening must have been astronomical. Boro did have to face a nervous few moments as Steaua launched a series of high balls at our defence, and there was a free-kick for the Romanians just outside the area, but they just couldn't come back. They weren't going to come back. The final whistle went and Boro were through to the final. The Riverside was bouncing, almost literally. I found myself hoping that Taylor Woodrow had made the structure good and strong as the fans bounced up and down in the stands. On the pitch the Boro team went as berserk as the fans, whilst the Bucharest players lay on the ground, desolate and inconsolable.

Finally we left the ground, stunned by what we had seen happen. I chanted hoarse songs into the night air as I went back to my car, then sat and grinned like a mentally unhinged man as I listened to Ali Brownlee on Century Radio talking about the game. They replayed the commentary from the final whistle and he had gone on a legendary rant about the Infant Hercules being forged from the Eston hills and everyone being invited back to his house for a parmo. I laughed all the way home, I think. If I'd been pulled over, I may well have been arrested even though a drop hadn't passed my lips. I was drunk on Boro.

The buzz would take a long time to wear off. We found out that we would be facing the Spanish team Sevilla FC in the final after they had beaten Schalke 04 by just one goal on aggregate in their semi-final. They had a reasonably unspectacular history with a smattering of minor successes, but weren't what one would consider a major European power. In my mind, I started to plot how I could get my sausage fingers on a ticket and get to the biggest game in Boro's history.

There were still four more league games (all away) to play before the UEFA Cup Final, which would be the last game of Boro's season. We didn't win another league game, as it happens, losing to Everton, drawing with Manchester United and Bolton then losing to Fulham on the closing day of the Premier League season. The game at Craven Cottage was notable for the squad that played that Sunday afternoon, with a team made entirely of home-grown players taking the field. Safety had been secured already (we finished fourteenth) and this was the fourth game in around eight days, catching up on all the league games that had been postponed left, right and centre due to the cup runs. The final would be Boro's 64th game of the season, and the first team players needed some rest, I'm sure.

It was well known in Boro circles that Steve Gibson had long harboured a dream to put out a home-grown team of local lads playing with pride and passion, so with the set of circumstances falling as fortuitously as they did, that chance was taken. By all accounts they did themselves proud against Fulham, despite losing 1-0.

And so, with 10th May approaching fast, I found myself running out of options. I read the tales of woe on internet forums about people who couldn't get a ticket for either love or money. The main problem seemed to be the disgracefully low number of tickets allocated to fans of each club. PSV's stadium in Eindhoven, the Philips Stadion, is about as big as the Riverside in terms of capacity, meaning only a maximum of 17,000 fans from each team could go. But this was before the neutral and corporate tickets were taken off the allocation, and once these were ring-fenced there were only 12,000 tickets given to each team for distribution. Bloody sickening; that's what that was. There were bound to be some disappointed fans, and I heard of people who had held season tickets from the Ayresome Park days not being able to get a ticket. Many decided that they would still travel to Holland, even without a ticket. They just wanted to be in Eindhoven when their team played in a European final. Just twenty years earlier they had nearly gone out of existence, so you can understand why they felt this way.

For me, I knew I had no chance and indeed no good right to get my hands on a ticket from the official allocation, so I resorted to the rather less-than-official routes being taken by many people, i.e. bidding for the hundreds of neutral tickets being put up for auction on the world-wide web. There were some ridiculous prices being asked for and bid, and I soon became disheartened and resigned myself to watching on TV. About a week before the match I luckily happened across a post on an internet messageboard by a chap who had secured two tickets for about £150 a piece on e-bay, and was willing to sell one of them to the first person who replied and who was able to offer a lift to Eindhoven. I then remembered that there was a chap at work who was a long-term season ticket holder and had managed to get a ticket and who had been talking about driving there on his own or with others, so I knew that in logistical terms at least, there were possibilities. I quickly and excitedly replied to the ticket seller, exchanged e-mail addresses, and the deal was done.

In the meantime I found myself getting involved in a weird little whirlwind of activism and media interest that sprang out of almost nothing. In the days before the final there was an announcement by the club that any victory parade around the town would take place the day after the final: i.e. on a Thursday. People at work and on the various forums were astonished at this bizarre line of thought. Firstly, it was a work and school day, and secondly many people would still be either travelling back from Holland by 'plane, train, car or even donkey convoy, or still over in the Netherlands nursing hangovers. Why wasn't it scheduled for the weekend?

I'm not quite sure how it happened, but I think I brought up the idea of an online petition to put forward the feelings of the fans.

Someone said, "Good idea", and suggested that I should go ahead and set one up, seeing as they are so easy to do. Before I knew it I had written up a petition begging the club to reconsider and started publicising it on the internet with the help of some willing supporters. Next thing I knew I was being e-mailed by reporters from the Gazette, appearing on the BBC Tees breakfast show and being interviewed by local TV news crews outside the Riverside.

In the end we got over 1,000 signatures on the petition in a few days, so I printed it off and took it to the stadium reception where a bored-looking receptionist promised to give it straight to the dustbin. Well, maybe someone did read it, to be fair, and probably noticed the news coverage of a fat bloke in a navy blue Boro shirt limping around the Riverside stadium clutching a ream of paper. They didn't show my interview on TV, the swines, but I did receive an e-mail from the PR department of MFC thanking me for my support (I wasn't sure if that was sarcasm or not) and setting out the reasons why they couldn't possibly move any victory parade, mainly because all the players were going straight on holiday and wouldn't be available. It all fizzled out and I was left feeling a little sheepish at having got caught up in a cause that was all about something that might not even happen. Some people even berated me for tempting fate by going on and on about victory parades. It had given me a buzz while it lasted, though. Infamy, infamy! I'll take it now, and any spare cake going!

With all that nonsense forgotten about, final preparations were made for the big drive to the game. The chap from work and the bloke who sold me the ticket (Work Chap and Ticket Bloke shall be their names from now on) were to drive down to Thirsk and we would all pile in my car for the epic drive. I had booked a channel crossing on the Eurotunnel for around lunchtime, giving us plenty of time to get up to Eindhoven from Calais. The six-hour drive to Folkestone on the English side meant we would have to leave at around 6am. The driving would be shared, and to save money on accommodation (even if we could have found any) we would drive straight back.

Preparations by the team were somewhat disrupted by the announcement, less than a week before the final, that Steve McClaren would be taking the vacant England manager's role at the end of the season. He had been in the running for a while, and after Big Phil Scolari had turned the FA down, McClaren had been seen as the next best choice. It wasn't great timing for the club, but there was little that could be done about it. The UEFA Cup Final would be McClaren's last game in charge of the Boro.

On the glorious, sunny morning of 10th May, 2006, Ticket Bloke and Work Chap turned up bright and early, resplendent in Boro shirts. Work Chap also wore sandals with socks, but as he was over the age of fifty I wasn't going to ridicule him for his fashion sense. I lost any superiority I may have had in the credibility stakes when I attached a tatty, Union-flag-backed Boro car flag to the rear passenger window of my blue Citroen Picasso. Well, it's not every day you set off to drive 1,000 miles in just over 24 hours to watch Middlesbrough play in a European Final is it, for God's sake?

The journey there was fine. It took about nine hours in total, as I had anticipated, and we arrived in the chocolate-box city of Eindhoven mid-afternoon. There were some lovely traditional buildings around, but large parts of the town were made up of brand new buildings and plazas full of mind-boggling modern art pieces. This isn't surprising when you realise that the city was devastated in the latter stages of the Second World War. The whole area was the focus for Operation Market Garden, the ill-fated push following D-Day that had been designed to bring the war to a finish before Christmas 1944, and reminded me of that wartime video game I'd played far too often. As we approached our destination on the flat Dutch motorways, we noticed a few familiar place names, such as Arnhem and Nijmegen, site of that bridge that was famously one too far. History was all around us.

We found parking alongside a large public open space by a main thoroughfare leading to the city centre and decided to walk from there, taking in the sights and sounds. We passed a parked coach bearing the name "FUCKER" in huge blue letters, much to our childish amusement, before passing through a few concrete underpasses and emerging near the stadium itself. We paused to take some photos standing across the street from the ground. It reminded me of a mini version of Cardiff's Millennium Stadium with the pillars in the corner, but there were a few little quirks such as the visible gaps (for ventilation, presumably) in the terracing in the corners.

As the game itself was still a good four or five hours away, we decided to try and find the Boro designated fan square, where there was supposedly entertainment laid on. We followed the few other Boro fans we saw milling around, but I was surprised to see that the Sevilla fans were more visible. As we passed one group of them, they held their arms out for hugs and handshakes, shouting the word, "Friend!" as they came. They seemed in great spirits.

Nearer the heart of the city we spied more Boro fans. Most of them were in great spirits of the alcohol kind, having arrived the night before via Flight Options jumbo jets or whatever they'd travelled in and then hitting the bars since breakfast. We stopped for a bite to eat in a McDonaldsh, as you do, marveling at the weird little sachets of mayonnaise handed to us for dipping our fries in, before heading further on to try and find the Boro square. We found it eventually, but didn't stay long. There were even more inebriated Teessiders spilling their beer all over the place and talking loudly. There was no malice, but it's never fun being the sober one at a party. We found a relatively quiet bar where we could find a table outside and enjoyed one beer each. We reflected on the drama that had brought us here and wondered what the last ninety minutes of this amazing season would bring.

Oh, what little we knew, eh?

As the time for action approached, we set off back for the stadium, joining the red and white-adorned stream of humanity heading for whatever destiny awaited. I bumped into one or two familiar faces on the way, and as we passed the stadium a bit of a hullaballoo erupted as the great Tony Mowbray was spotted entering the stadium. At the corner we had passed earlier, Work Chap split from our little group to take his place in the Boro end of the ground. That left Ticket Bloke and me to worry about whether our £150 quid tickets were genuine or not. We joined the queue for our designated turnstile at the side of the stadium and nervously inched forward. We were mixed in with fans of both teams, all of whom had probably had to buy their tickets through unofficial channels. There was no hint of trouble, which was nice. The few Spaniards who spoke English wished us luck with broad smiles.

We got in, thank the Gods, and after climbing the stairs I was initially quite alarmed at how steep the terracing was, but then realised that we had got our hands on some prime tickets. We were just to the right of the half-way line, towards the end of the ground housing the official Sevilla contingent. They were already creating a hell of a racket and passing a huge surfer banner over their heads. The smaller Boro surfer came out at the other end, but was held somewhat askew. A large proportion of the fans were obviously now struggling to function after a day in the sun and on the lash. A few attempts to get chants and songs going fizzled out fairly quickly.

And then it was time for the game. The usual pomp and ceremony of a European final was unleashed, with fireworks and dancers and dancing hippos galore, and then the game kicked off. We had Mark Schwarzer back in goal, wearing a *Phantom of the Opera*-style plastic protective face-mask, but McClaren seemed to have set the team up to be defensive, and this invited Sevilla pressure from the off. Their full-backs had a lot of the ball and set up wave after wave of attacks. Boro just couldn't get into it, and it was no surprise when the Spanish side took the lead in the 26th minute with a header by Fabiano, set up by a long, raking cross from right full-back.

Boro avoided conceding any more goals until half-time at least, and then the manager decided to change things. The hero of the last two rounds, Maccarone, was brought on at half time and we finally started to threaten the Sevilla goal. Viduka had a great chance to level after Riggott headed a free-kick back across goal, but the goalie saved from point-blank range. A pivotal moment came with about 14 minutes left. Viduka went down under a challenge in the area as he chased a long ball but the ref waved play on. It looked a stone-waller from up where I was watching, and the Boro fans were furious. As is often the way with these games, Sevilla scored their second only two minutes later, and in my heart of hearts, I knew it was over. There was no way that we could come back from this. Sevilla were too good, and there just wasn't enough time.

Two more goals came in the last five minutes, rubbing it in and breaking Boro hearts. The Sevilla fans around us were in ecstasy. They knew that they would win their first trophy in nearly 60 years. I wanted to leave after the third went in, but Ticket Bloke insisted on staying until the horribly bitter end. We stayed long enough to applaud our team off the pitch, but I couldn't bear to watch the Spaniards lift that trophy and I descended the stairs as quickly as I could, shaking a few Spanish hands offered to me as I left. I didn't have any truck with them. It was their turn, as it had been our turn in Cardiff in 2004.

After a call on my mobile we located the dejected form of Work Chap shuffling in his sandals away from the ground. We all shuffled back to the car and set straight off for Calais, hoping to catch an early-morning crossing back to England's green and pleasant land. Very few words were spoken as we drove through Holland. We got a bit lost in Belgium, but before long we were back on the train that goes deep under the English Channel, worn out and pretty stunned by what we had witnessed.

The English side of the return journey was a tortuous slog. Everyone was shattered but couldn't sleep when they were off driving duty. I didn't dare sleep as I was sure Work Chap was going to drift off at any moment behind the wheel. We made it home safely, at least, and I headed straight to bed. At least I didn't have to worry about making it to a victory parade now.

And that was that. The season was over. The adventures had ended, and our most successful manager of all time was now leaving to coach the national team. The team was getting old and the future was very, very uncertain. Where did we go from here? We hadn't qualified for Europe this time round, so maybe consolidation was on the cards. Most Boro fans hoped we could find a high-profile manager to take us to that next level where we could compete for and maybe even win trophies like the UEFA Cup on a regular basis.

Over to you, Mr. Gibson...

Epilogue

This is the end, my friends...

And so, dear reader, (assuming that you've stuck with me and my meandering, melancholy musings) we have reached the end of my tale. The UEFA Cup final in Eindhoven, in all its glorious horror, seems an appropriate place for me to conclude what is essentially the story of Boro's Golden Decade from the point of view of an outsider. Quite frankly I can't see this period being surpassed. Ever.

I feel exceedingly fortunate to have been around for it all. When I went to my first Boro match at Ayresome Park, that testimonial against Manchester United back in 1994, I could never have imagined what lay in store. There were cup runs galore, dramatic semi-finals, nail-depleting relegation battles both successful and doomed, triumphant cup finals, hammerings and batterings both given and suffered, hero-worshipped midfielders and big-time Charlie strikers, rookie managers and stabilising old hands, rain, snow, wind and around a dozen different home and away strip combinations bearing the red lion rampant on the circular badge. If someone wrote this tale as a piece of fiction or a film script, they'd surely be laughed out of town.

Since that day in May 2006 a lot has happened and so much has changed. There was surprise and no little disappointment in the direction chosen by the club after McClaren's departure. There had been talk of managers like Martin O'Neill and Oliver Hitzfeld coming to take the reins, but Gibson decided to go with a player who had covered himself in glory in the previous few seasons and the only captain to ever lift a trophy over his head in a Middlesbrough shirt. Gareth Southgate is undoubtedly an intelligent and decent man who deserves great respect, but it may have been too soon for him to step up from playing for to managing a Premier League football team.

The Afonso Alves debacle was an expensive mistake, and signaled a final flourish in the casino of gambling with big-money signings. There was a bit of a cup run in the FA Cup, but the nature of the home defeat to Cardiff in the quarter final, allied to the relative weakness of the other teams left in the competition, left a sour taste for many people. With crowds continuing to dwindle, relegation loomed large and became a reality only a matter of seasons after Eindhoven. It was all thoroughly depressing. The club hadn't kicked on from appearing in their first European final; if anything they'd gone backwards. All the good (read expensive) players left. It seemed the club were cutting their cloth to suit, and arguments about who was to blame soon flared up. The club were blamed for their lack of ambition and the fans were blamed for not attending the matches. It became something of a Catch-22 situation. There is something slightly insane about supporting Boro, of course.

Despite a decent start to the season and with Boro in a promotion spot at the time, Southgate gave way to Strachan in September 2009. "False position - papering over the cracks," as the middle-aged, serial grumblers of the East Stand like to say, amongst other inspiring *bons mots*. Strachan brought in Scots and Scottish-based players galore at the beginning of the next season, but despite the bookies making Boro favourites to win the Championship, the team that looked good on tartan paper played like a bunch of skirted Jessies on the pitch and by Christmas were flirting with the kind of humiliation suffered by Leeds and Man City in the last few years. League One would not have been fun, even if one or two fans suggested it might just work as some kind of cleansing catharsis. Happily, that was never going to be allowed to happen and Strachan was replaced by the man who had replaced him at Celtic: Tony Mowbray.

Mowbray turned us around, steered us to safety and went about pruning the team down to a lean, mean footballing machine. As I write, he has the team playing well and challenging for automatic promotion. It goes without saying that he is the most popular manager at Boro for a long time. He is from Middlesbrough (well, Saltburn-by-the-Sea, but it's close enough) and he was a legend as a player. He was the one that provoked talk of flights to the moon and so on, and was also part of that heroic bunch of lads who trained on public parkland when the club were dangerously close to going out of existence in 1986. He is an honest and sharp-minded man who knows what Boro are all about, and fans have been saying he should be our manager for quite a few years now. There's a long way yet to go, but there is definitely a feeling that things are finally going the right way again.

As I've said, whatever happens in the future, I just can't see it surpassing the heady, crazy times experienced between 1995 and 2006. I've also said that I felt fortunate to climb on board the Boro bandwagon when I did, but I think Boro fans in general should feel lucky that they experienced what they did. The club rose from the ashes just twenty five years ago and have been on one hell of a journey, culminating in the 2006 UEFA Cup final. This period of prosperity wasn't a God-given right, but it wouldn't have been possible without the vision and investment of one Steve Gibson. Not many teams of comparable size and from similar provincial towns have had such sustained and exciting days in the sun. I think there is also some truth in the old adage that to enjoy the highs you need to experience the lows.

And if we start to get depressed about how the good times looked to have ended in the years since Eindhoven, we can look back with the benefit of hindsight and see that there really had to be an adjustment to a slimmer, more economical model of club football. There are a handful of teams at the top with Arab, American and Russian money who Hoover up all the rest of the TV money thanks to the way things have been nicely fixed in the last twenty years, and the rest have to scrap over the crumbs being brushed from the table. Gibson has made sure that we still have a functioning club at least, whilst many others are counting the cost of careless borrowing and profligate spending on overpaid tattooed tossers who have little concept of reality. Thanks a lot, Rupert. Thanks a bloody bunch.

Deep breaths…

As for me, well 2006 was a year that saw another big change for me. In July I was offered a job in the Middle East and spent a year in Dubai with my family, and I've already written the book about that particular period. I've been in and out of the country since then, fighting against health problems and bleak economic times, but have always had my eyes and ears out for the Boro results, getting to at least one or two matches a season. I fear that if I don't keep taking my son to the Riverside he will start supporting Newcastle or Leeds. I remember that he wavered momentarily when Viduka went to the Geordies, but I managed to steer him away from such folly without having to resort to violence.

What else is there left to say? Not a lot. Whether or not anyone thinks this has all just been an attempt to justify or ingratiate myself, I hope it's been an entertaining account of Middlesbrough Football Club's recent history. I've enjoyed going through it all again, having my memory jogged by the results, be they victories, defeats or draws. I make no apologies and have no regrets about the path I chose back in the mid 1990s. I could have easily and lazily stuck with the successful team I followed as a kid, but where would the fun have been in that?

Thanks for the ride, Boro.

Christopher Combe - December 2011